When My Well Ran Dry

by

Racquel D. Innis-Shelton, MD

DORRANCE
PUBLISHING CO
EST. 1920
PITTSBURGH, PENNSYLVANIA 15238

The contents of this work including, but not limited to, the accuracy of events, people, and places depicted; opinions expressed; permission to use previously published materials included; and any advice given or actions advocated are solely the responsibility of the author, who assumes all liability for said work and indemnifies the publisher against any claims stemming from publication of the work.

Dorrance Publishing Co
585 Alpha Drive
Suite 103
Pittsburgh, PA 15238
Visit our website at *www.dorrancebookstore.com*

ISBN: 978-1-4349-2866-5
eISBN: 978-1-4349-2218-2

Dedication

I dedicate this book to my mother, who has always been there to dry my every tear and offer guidance through every endeavor. She not only encourages me to fly, but to soar with grace. I also dedicate this to my dear husband. Paradoxically, without your tenacity, my journey to self may have never occurred.

Preface

*W*hat do you do when you feel like you've lost everything? When you feel like you are living in the middle of a dried up wasteland where there is no hope and your soul is desolate. How do you crawl out of a deep, dark hole of despair? Someone once told me, "pain is pain". There is so much truth in this simple phrase. Pain is all the same, it just comes in many forms. Maybe you were deeply betrayed, sexually abused, beaten by a spouse, or buried a loved one after an untimely death. It all hurts. Even if you're just simply overwhelmed with your current life circumstance and see no way out…that hurts too. I'm here to tell you that you're not alone, and there is a way out. Every human being experiences some type of severe emotional pain at some point in their lives.

My pain has to do with my husband of almost seventeen years. He left me alone with four children between the ages of two to eleven, a demanding career, and a shattered self-esteem. My story is about how I overcame the grief of his rejection. For a while, I asked God daily why I was going through such a painful separation from a man I lived with my entire adult life. Why only now, after all the schooling was done and all the kids are born, would something like this occur? Why only now, when we were finally set in our careers would turmoil hit us from out of nowhere? Well, maybe it was so I could write this book. Without the transformation within me that came out of my painful marital strife, I would not have anything to share. I hope that my story gives you hope, and helps you to overcome whatever grief you may be dealing with.

"When the well is dry,
we know the value of water"
—Benjamin Franklin

Chapter One:
Grief

*U*nlike physical injury which can be bandaged, emotional injury requires special care and time in order to be properly soothed. Severe pain warrants a grieving period, there is something that is lost; a person, pride, dignity, self-worth, or a dream. The damage requires you to go through certain stages in order to heal.

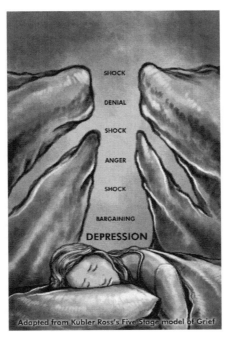

Adapted from Kubler Ross's Five Stage model of Grief

Stages:

Shock/Disbelief: emotionally stunned that the event has occurred

Denial: routine behavior continued as though loved one is still there

Anger: angry at oneself, lost loved one, or situation

Bargaining: make a deal to change the situation (sometimes with God)

Depression: profound sadness over loss

Acceptance and Hope: acceptance that life has changed, but life will go on.[1]

For me, these stages did not seem to occur in any perfect order, and some of them I may have gone through more than once. Undoubtedly, I experienced each one of these stages along my journey through grief, at one point or another.

My husband and I are both physicians. We used to be a military family. We moved ten times within the first fifteen years of marriage, had four children, and both he and I have gone through several different career changes. We had the typical marital strife, but with our stressful schedules, little arguments about little things turned into big arguments about nothing. Then around year thirteen, he drew away from me slowly, and then told me he did not love me anymore and no longer wanted to be married. This was in the midst of a huge career move for me, which initially made me hostile and angry. Then as he began to take real steps to permanently separate our lives. I became terrified, desperate, and grief-stricken.

Grief can take you into a deep dark hole of despair. After going there myself, I can see how some people, who feel like they have no way out of their circumstance, fall into self-destructive behavior or even contemplate suicide in extreme cases. Me, being a physician, should know better, but yes...even I too, have gone there in my thinking. There were moments when I thought to myself, "Ah hell, I can't take this anymore... I'm done!" I needed a way out. I most often felt this way when, emotionally, my pain was so severe that I physically felt like my innards were being ripped out of me, twisted, and strangled at gut-level. Much like the hole that Bella describes when Edward leaves her in Stephenie Meyer's second book of the Twilight series, *New Moon*[2]; it really felt as if someone punched a hole in my chest, knocking all the wind out of me, and then stabbed a jagged-edged dagger through my heart, which was then slowly twisted in deeper and deeper until I felt that my entire self would be swallowed up into an abyss of eternal pain and darkness. One too many nights I would cry so hard until I felt that anguish was literally gripping me by the throat from the inside out. I felt as though I'd either just stop breathing, burst, or that my brain would explode from all the built-up pressure inside. I would find myself crawling around on my bedroom floor, gasping for breath, only to fall asleep, curled up in a fetal position.

Sorrow this deep can lead you to pray to God that He just wouldn't allow you to open your eyes the next morning. I would ask God to have mercy on me and relieve me from my misery by not letting me wake up to this much sorrow, not one more day. But I **would** open my eyes the next morning, full of melancholy and more fatigued than the day before as though I'd never slept a wink. It would take every ounce of strength I had to drag myself out of bed, starting every day feeling like a horse that'd been rode hard and put up wet. It took what seemed like a very long time for me to finally decide that I never wanted to have such profound sadness ever again.

Depression

Chapter Two:
Climbing Out of the Deep Hole of Grief

*A*s I was gripped by grief, and the reality of my loss settled in, it felt as though there would be no end to what had become sheer lunacy. For months, I was absolutely convinced that this must all be a mistake. Surely I wasn't living this life that was set before me. Surely this was someone else's life and not mine. But it was my life and it was real. I started to feel hopeless. The plan I'd made for my life was abruptly altered by someone else's choices, over which I had no control. To me, it felt that everything I'd grown to depend on was all a lie; my dreams for the future were all shattered. I felt deeply betrayed. Life can become completely meaningless when you have the belief that you have absolutely no power to change an unbearable life circumstance. This is the state in which I was living.

My family along with a few friends I'd kept in touch with and new ones I'd made, tried their best to support me, but with all their effort, I was barely hanging on by a thin thread. I managed to exist and keep up a good front so the outside world would not figure out how broken I was inside. I was barely existing. I wanted to thrive again, to be happy. But how? Where would I start? I felt like I was mentally, emotionally, and physically stuck in a sea of quick sand with no dangling branches to reach for.

In the beginning, cliché phrases like, "things will get better" or "you'll be fine" seemed nebulous and intangible. How exactly? How were things really going to just "get better"? Something within me knew that I had to deal with this life shock and get out of my own funk, but the specific steps I needed to take to achieve true and sustained happiness remained an enigma for years. One of my sisters, who, by the way, should really wear a cape, gold bangles and fly around in an invisible jet, would say, "Girlfriend, you just have to shake that off and move the hell on!" Well, I shook, but nothing happened. She owns a medical practice with her husband, who is recovering from cancer. She has an autistic child, always has high spirits, and never misses a beat. But not even she, my eternal cheerleader, nor anyone else by themselves, could take my pain away. I would feel almost guilty complaining to her with all that she deals with in her regular life. After talking with her, I would try to brainwash myself into thinking that I was okay, and that everything would work out "just fine", whatever "just fine" was. If there was a new definition of living without my husband, I had no ability to tell what that would even look like. It wouldn't take long for me to be defeated by my new reality, feel barren, hollowed out from my core, bewildered, and very much alone. When the ties to my husband were severed, I felt maimed. My ego was severely injured. I felt nameless without him. I didn't even feel like I should carry his name. So where was I...somewhere in between my father's name and my husband's name? My father had been dead for several years so in whose house did I truly belong? I felt like I no longer belonged anywhere. I felt like I was left adrift in some type of middle world–unclaimed, and unwanted. I was in a very dark place.

Each minute of the day remained a struggle for two solid years. I would pray for complicated patient cases or a busy workday, so I wouldn't have to ruminate about my own hopelessness or listen to the constant replay in my mind of what I thought must have gone wrong. When my busy day was over, pain and sadness were always waiting for me on the other side of the door. The turmoil was a continuous and ongoing mental struggle. Quiet times, leaving work, and car rides home were torturous. It's as though a looming evil force was whispering to me when I was all alone, *"You can just drive off a cliff, or do something terminal now, while the kids are not with you or while they're sleeping."* Can you believe there was a small part of me that wanted to listen? I so desperately wanted to be free of my pain. I didn't feel good enough for anything. I felt like a failure.

I started to wonder how other people deal with deep pain. I think it's easy to run to mind-numbing activities during times of grief as some type of a self-preservation coping mechanism or what may seem like the only way "out". When the pain is so great that your only hope of escape is to either turn to drugs/alcohol or even contemplate ending your life, that's when you're in trouble. These are the times when you need help fast. You need to find your own reason to live or something to live for. These are the times when we are most vulnerable, and may become self-destructive in order to escape from what seems like an otherwise inescapable pain. I could identify with these feelings at my darkest hours.

Fortunately, I had my children and my job to get me out of bed every day even though at times I was nearly paralyzed with grief. I consider myself quite lucky to be able to stay away from destructive behavior and, with a lot of help, found a way to climb out of the depths of my own personal hell. It was during the dark times when I learned what it really meant to pray. Not only did I learn how to pray, but I also learned how to read the Bible and how to look deep within myself to find answers to life's most difficult questions. I don't know what your faith is or if you have one. I happen to follow the teachings of Jesus Christ. The message of Christ has come through many different forms and many different cultures. If you look deeply at the major religions of the world, the messages are quite similar. God is in all of our lives in one way or another, and we are meant to love one another. I think because Adam and Jesus (the Son) were human males, we traditionally refer to God as a male figure as well. I refer to God in this book as "He" or "Him", but who really knows how to characterize the massive force that breathes life into this world. Can you contain such force in a single word? Just one word seems too small. God is so....infinite. Whatever your faith is, cling to it and nurture it like you never have before. Learning to pray literally saved my life and gave a mother back to my children who would have been devastated to grow up without one. The changes that occurred within me as my life took on a new and unexpected path, seemed to take an eternity. The solutions did not come overnight. I had no choice but to embark upon a slow journey to recovery.

Shock/Disbelief

Chapter Three:
Recovering from Hurt is a Slow Process

*R*ecovering from deep hurt can be a daily, and often, minute-by-minute challenge. From the moment you awaken, you face ruminating thoughts of fear and defeat. You want to do something, but there's nothing to do. The things you may tend to do in this state are likely not based on any level-headed thought and more likely to be harmful or destructive than they are to be helpful. But it constantly nags at you from the inside out—your life is terribly wrong and you just want to feel better. This circular treadmill of rumination leads to nowhere. It only reinforces how bad you feel about yourself and your hopeless circumstance. This treadmill lead me down into a deeper path of despair, one without any effective solutions. While I was grieving the loss of my husband, there were very few good moments. Random innocent phrases or constant reminders of his absence triggered my "emptiness" button, and the hurt returned full force. I often found myself curled up in bed under the covers, wanting to die.

When my husband left, I thought my life was over. Since I can remember, I wanted to grow up, get married, be either a successful actress or a doctor, and have kids...in that order. Well I did those things (minus the successful actress), but I didn't realize that my list was lacking a few fundamental milestones. I was twenty-three years old when I got married, and quickly became accustomed to being a married woman. Most of what I did on a daily basis for all of my adult life centered around my husband, job, and children. I started to question the image of myself that I identified with. Without the marriage, who was I? What did I even like to do? I had no idea, and definitely didn't want to do, whatever it was, alone. Why did I feel like without my husband, I had no life? Maybe it was shallow thinking on my part. I don't know. But deep down I suddenly felt completely out-of-place and off-balance.

Unfortunately, and without knowing, I'd defined myself by my marital status and now felt as though I failed a primary life goal. I was severely disappointed. It was not for some time that I realized I made the fatal mistake of letting go of old friends and hobbies in order to devote my full attention to my career and family. I'd groomed myself to believe that my identity as wife, mother, doctor were my life's fundamental measures of accomplishment. The person who was just simply me, got lost under all of those titles. I didn't know who I was supposed to be anymore. Maybe that was a big part of the problem, I was trying to figure out who I was "supposed" to be (and I'm not exactly sure who defines that) instead of the person that I actually was? Why, on earth, did I feel like I no longer had an identity? Who was I before I became all those other people, with all those other titles? I couldn't remember.

I thought my pain and suffering over this loss would linger on for a lifetime, and I would literally die from a broken heart. I would think, *Oh, dear God, why me? What have I done to deserve this?* I thought, maybe this is my lot in life, punishment for my past sins. Then I would repent for my every wrong doing. I even went back to events from second grade. I begged forgiveness from anyone who I'd ever hurt or shunned. I promised God that I would become a perfect human if He'd just turn this all around. Who was I kidding? I guess this was the *"bargaining"* phase of my grief state. In almost the same breath, I would then feel guilty. I felt like a spoiled, whiny brat wanting to have my way. I wanted to smack my own self, and just snap out of it. What right have I to ask, *Why me?* Do thirty year olds with end-stage cancer ask, "Why me?" Well, maybe they do at some point, but people with cancer may actually die with unbearable physical pain. I can live through my pain. So with that in mind, I would temporarily silence myself and stop complaining.

Ultimately, what I've found is that time really does heal all wounds. But it has to pass…time, that is. My mother always says, "This too shall pass". How true those words are as life unfolds. Every transient minute transitions to the next. Every day is a new day with new choices to make. What you do with time as it passes by, is your choice. Don't make the mistake I initially did, wishing you'd have some sub-lethal car accident that would render you comatose on a ventilator for six months, and when you wake up, your loving husband would be right back at your side, ready to scoop you up and take care of you once more. That sounds so silly now. At the time, I wanted to crawl under a rock and only climb out after the storm had blown over and order was restored. I'd adopted a fairytale mode of thinking, wanting something… anything, to come along and save the day. I honestly wanted to just blink my eyes like a genie and have all of it wisp away. But this wasn't a bad dream to wake from. It was real. What was happening to us revealed years of deep seated, stored resentments that no snap of the finger could fix overnight. I did not know how to fight what was coming at me and I suffered the misconception that if I didn't have my husband by my side, I would be destined to a life of loneliness and unhappiness. I saw no way out of this and thought my unhappiness would be a permanent state for the next forty plus years. Oh "pity, pity", and "woe is me" were behind my every thought.

One morning at breakfast, my teenage son read aloud some pearls of wisdom he found on one of his cell phone app sites. The one that caught my attention was, "If you're unhappy with your life, then change something." I pondered this for a while. Could it be possible that I had the power to make a change that would make this pain go away? The idea of full recovery from my situation, without a miracle, was inconceivable at the time, but if I didn't make some type of change, sorrow would consume me forever, and my children deserved more out of life that an emotionally catatonic mother. But how, really? I figured I could at least change one thing…probably even two or three things to move toward happiness.

Deep down inside I knew very well, that when you sit in a corner and do nothing, nothing will happen. Like the pile of old toys in my garage that I don't want to sort through, or the terminally unpacked boxes that moved with us through each military station, things can stay the same for years if you don't tend to them. Since I did not want to remain sad for years, I knew I had to actively take part in healing myself, I just had no idea how to do it. What I needed was courage, but hiding under a rock sounded much more appealing. Mastin Kipp of TheDailyLove.com, once highlit a definition of courage from the Merriam Webster Collegiate Dictionary that caught my eye.

Courage: cour•age *noun* \'kər-ij, 'kə-rij\
implies firmness of mind and will in the face of danger or extreme difficulty.

Yeah. I needed a good dose of that alright.

Chapter Four:
The Shock of It All...
Am I Really a Single Parent Now?

*F*or the first couple of years, I remained severely broken-hearted, but tried to tackle my life's tasks head on and busied myself with getting some organization back in my life. While bawling on the inside, I learned how to do several things I never did well before. Keeping up with homework, school, an unruly Labarador Retriever, bedtime stories, and sports schedules as the only adult and licensed driver in the house, while staying on top of your own career is damn near an impossible feat. You have to recruit friends, break things off in little chunks, and stick them in at odd hours of the day. I learned how to grocery shop and how to cook. (I was the youngest in my own family and didn't really learn these types of things well. My husband did much of these things and when he left, I realized how much I had to learn). To my surprise, I found it very easy to splash different marinades on meat, stick 'em on the grill, microwave oven bags of rice and veggies, and have a well-balanced dinner on the table in about forty-five minutes flat. It beat fast food and created family time at the dinner table. I made the crock pot my new BFF (best friend for life), became a master of a few set-it-and-forget-it meals, and learned how to save dollars by couponing. Couponing is actually a real art. It's worth the effort, especially if you have to suddenly make do on a single income. It's so difficult to feel strong if you're flat broke. As far as work is concerned, I really have a ten to twelve hour per day career, but I leave my job after eight hours to take care of my children. Every day, I'd have to figure how to stick a couple of extra non-direct patient care work either into the late night, early morning, or weekend hours. That made this doctor mama a very pooped puppy. I would fall out every night only to become engulfed in the throes of depression and worried excessantly over what type of future I would be able to provide for my children. I found it difficult to conduct daily life in a twenty-four hour period. I was completely overwhelmed most of the time and perpetually exhausted. My children's busy schedules and my demanding career kept me physically moving around even when I was emotionally absent. My children would not allow me to remain emotionally absent for long periods of time. Intermittently, they would say sweet things, tell funny stories, or present me with dilemmas that would force me to provide them with parental guidance and motherly wisdom. If it weren't for not wanting to embarrass them as I dropped them off at school, I'd likely not even comb my hair most days, settling for the wanton, disheveled look. I wish my mama had warned me on how to avoid this type of predicament. But even the best of us end up in unplanned circumstances. It seems to be a part of human life that manifests in so many different ways. Everyone has some type of life challenge. I was convinced that this was my cross to bear.

Eventually, I figured out how to accomplish the mechanical parts of daily life, but I still had not answered the question of how to really cope with all aspects of my new fate. What steps do you take to *really* feel like you are living, not just existing after a devastating event? How do you enjoy life despite the turmoil you're living through? People continued to tell me things like *"It'll get better,"* or *"It will work out,"*. But I still couldn't figure out how to do any more than just muddle through every day? If this too shall pass...would it just go ahead and pass already?

As it turns out, it all does pass, but it seems to take F-O-R-E-V-E-R. The grubby uncomfortable parts of the grief process can't be avoided or fast-forwarded through; they actually must be conquered. I started to consider very small accomplishments a victory. I celebrated being able to laugh a real laugh, or go a day without crying. I grasped at new coping mechanisms to help me through the anticipated "next time" sadness would come to rear it's ugly head. I chose different reading materials each equipped with some new tool that would get me through another day or teach me a skill set that I would use at a later date. I didn't realize what I was doing at the time, but I was taking a step-by-step journey into wellness. Nothing I learned on this journey was a waste. Each day needed to happen to get me one foot closer to climbing out of my own personal hole of despair. Each day was a victory that put me one step forward, along the path that was set before me.

Chapter Five:
What Could this All Possibly Mean?

*I*f you are currently in a hole, remember the words, "this too shall pass". Just hold on one day at a time. There is some purpose hidden in what you're going through. Search for the purpose and focus on it. God wants you to use this grief for some reason. This is the way we grow. Sometimes this can feel like a minute-by-minute struggle. When it is this severe, pray to get through to the next minute. You won't blow up or disintegrate, trust me. You'll be surprised, but spontaneous disintegration never occurs. Never do anything illegal or make a stupid move you'll one day live to regret. If anger is involved, you'll be completely closed to how God wants you to use your grief as fuel to ignite some act of good that may help many more people than you would have ever come in contact with, had you never experience the grief yourself. When I was angriest, I could see how some women could resort to smashing their mate's precious car windows or showing up at his job to expose him to all who think he is so fantastic for the true cad he may be behind closed doors. Even though you may think it to be a reasonable plan of revenge, please don't do it. Never do or say things you may regret. Just keep your immediate thoughts to yourself, hold your tongue, and find another outlet for your anger until you can come up with constructive solutions. Men can be quite sensitive. They are protective of their egos and become quickly unforgiving of any attack against it. My anger against my husband allowed me to hurl some not so flattering words at him, during this time. I lost all control of my emotions. My choice to remain angry did nothing for me or my relationship. My choice of words did nothing to bring my husband closer to me, and in fact, made a bad situation, even worse. I wish that I'd learned to manage my emotions earlier in life. I wish that I could have learned to look ahead and think to myself, "okay, if I exercise "*a*" emotion, then "*b*" will happen, but if I exercise "*c*" emotion then "*d*" will happen...then choose which emotion to display based on whichever outcome I desired to achieve.

Have you ever watched the game show, *Let's make a Deal?* A group of contestants are given the option to pick a secret prize behind a line of different colored curtains. No one knows what's behind each curtain. They just pick a color and get whatever they get. If the contestant chooses whatever is behind the yellow curtain, for example, they may win a luxury cruise, but if they choose what is behind the blue curtain, they get a weekend with ma, pa kettle, a pitchfork, and a donkey. I would say picking the blue curtain would be a poor choice. Unlike the curtains in *Let's Make a Deal*, we're not completely blind to what is behind the curtains of life, and can exercise some insight to predict the outcome that will occur if we choose to exercise certain emotions at inopportune times. Sometimes, we choose the wrong emotion anyway, because we feel that we are right and absolutely must be heard, validated and vindicated. But what do you win? When we exercise bad behavior in a relationship, especially one that is unstable, it is relatively easy to be placed in a box of no return and only appear to be the bitter, jilted ex—-turned lunatic. Hold your head up high and hurl thoughts of revenge down in the gutter. This type of behavior is beneath you, and ultimately, you would lose more than you hoped to gain. You'll feel so much better if you handle the situation with dignity. You may have to bite your lip, but muster up all the dignity you can find in these situations and you won't have to look back with the regret of having compromised yourself.

It's very difficult to *not* fight a problem head on, when attacked. I felt like everything was being stolen from me by a thief in the night, and I was defenseless. I was left to just "deal with it" and fend for myself. I was filled with thoughts of *I can't believe he would just get up and leave me with all this.... How could he..?*, and so on and so forth. I had to learn to dig up every ounce of restrain to contain my wits about me, and learn to *fight* in a different type of way. I had to learn how to not be anything less than what would be acceptable in God's eyes. I thought of Dr. Martin Luther King, Jr. and Mahatma Gandhi, who did not fight head on with guns or fists, but with unwavering faith, and words of love for human dignity. I had to acquire a reverence for self, beyond myself, that would always remain non-negotiable. So many things I thought were true in this world, turned out to be only a surface view. My experience showed me the ugliness that can lie beneath shiny surfaces. It was a rude awakening. Things I thought I could always rely on simply vanished into thin air as though they never existed. My husband began to behave as though there was never an "us", like I made up our love affair. Like I made up our life. All of a sudden he could not recall one good memory from our many years together, not one. I thought, *Huh?! Has he been drugged? How can such treachery be allowed????* This blatant slap in the face opened up a whole new way of "schooling" for me. I've never had to do anything more difficult, than scrape up my bottom jaw off the floor of my own personal hell hole and learn to "do life" all over again. This time, I was determined to do it with my eyes wide open.

Anger

Chapter Six:
How I Dealt with the Extremes of Anger

*A*fter a while, sadness began to alternate with extreme anger. I was so angry at him for having stolen from me the future I'd envisioned for us and our children. It was like having the rug pulled out from under my foothold on life. Around this time, a very good friend of mine encouraged me to pick up running. I hadn't run in a long time, so she advised me to start slow with an online program called "From Couch to 5K." Well, I had nothing to lose from this. So, like Forest Gump, I just started running. While running, I would think of every thought that was hurtful and every word from my husband's mouth that made me angry or hurt my feelings. As I pounded the pavement, I imagined each painful memory being squashed under my feet, including my husband's face at times. This was extremely gratifying and even purging. By the end of each run, I consistently felt more calm and cleansed of bad feelings. It's as though I left a string of bad thoughts trailing behind me. Painful memories would slowly be released from me with each drop of sweat that poured off my body. I soon became addicted to the euphoric, purified, and at-ease feeling that running would bring. Even though I felt too tired to even walk when I started, I felt better when I got the hang of running. I also looked better and was physically stronger and less fatigued. The energy I gained from my newfound sport was contagious, and soon, everyone around me was becoming more physically active. Even my superwoman sister invested in a pair of running shoes and hit the marathon trail.

Running became an extremely effective way for me to physically release emotionally pent-up frustrations. I found that it worked a lot better than tears, which often just made me feel worse. Reluctantly, I learned that any climb out of the grief hole can only happen one step at a time. In order for you to grow, you can't just cover your head and try to go through life with your eyes closed; it just won't blow over.

Change and growth are dynamic. You have to open your eyes and see the world as it changes with you. The person who comes out of that hole will be stronger, more beautiful, and wiser than the one who fell in.

Denial

Chapter Seven:
What Happened to Me While
I Waited for a Lightning Bolt?

I kept hoping that a lightning bolt would strike some sense into my husband, like a smite directly from the hand of God Himself. I was still absolutely convinced that this must be a mistake. He must have been given some

type of amnesia drug on his last military tour, because this was not us. This story was not our life, but should instead be a sad movie. After searching through the typical oh-is-there-another- -woman suspicion, I was convinced that he must be going through a midlife crisis...and this was all transient. I'm ashamed to say that I held on to that notion for more than two years (yes, unlike many, I am extremely patient...just call me Job). I dragged my feet obnoxiously on divorce proceedings...all while waiting for my miracle event that would wake my husband up out of his stuporous coma...but it didn't happen. Early on, we'd roller-coaster back and forth, but after a while, he made his plan for terminal separation quite clear. Each time I would call him, wanting to talk, he would be cold, callous, and downright mean. Rejection after rejection turned me into a shell of my former self. I could not understand how a person who proclaimed undying love to me for a decade could flip the switch like this and *really mean it?* He must have had this planned for a while without letting me in on it. To me, the thought of living separately never crossed my mind as a possibility for our future. Just one year before our move, he gave me a beautiful card that said how he wanted nothing more than to grow old with me. Three weeks before he told me to get a lawyer, he sent two dozen roses for Valentine's day. Huh? Wha' happen'? I really thought we'd stay married forever.

This new information he presented seemed to come out of left field leaving me no time to prepare for it. By the time he revealed his level of unhappiness, his mind was not open to any workable solution; it was already made up to leave. I thought that was so unfair. I kept wondering why on earth would he not sit down and talk to me before it came to this. I don't know. Maybe he didn't know how to talk to me. I don't know. Either way, I was really a wreck, and I prayed to God repeatedly to deliver me from this strife. Remembering my son's app pearl about change, I knew that if something didn't change, I could remain this way for years, dwelling on the same old sad love song and buried in "why me" and "how could he". I knew I did not want to wake up one day in my eighties and realize that my life was only about pity and sorrow. Deep down, I knew that I had way too many other blessings in my life to remain sad over something that was obviously out of my control. For two years straight, I'd prayed for God to change my husband, but that got me nowhere. One day I realized that I'd given this relationship that I had (or didn't have) with my husband far too much power over my life. This is when I decided to change my prayer focus. A dear friend of mine often says that you should never ask God to change anyone, unless you first ask Him to change you first. So, I started to ask God to change me instead. This turn made a world of difference.

It's funny how, when you face turmoil, you come to realize that age-old sayings, cliché's, and wives-tales, actually have sound truth to them and have trickled down through history because they consist of universal truths that transcend time, place, and culture. You will hear me refer to them at several times in this book. Many of them associated with my own personal, as Oprah

Winfrey calls them, "Aha" moments. It's funny that you can hear something all of your life, but when put in a particular context and at a particular season in your life, the meaning can be completely different. I believe you have to be open and willing to receive a message; otherwise, you may not even be able to recognize the message something contains, at all. You also hear things differently at different times in your life, not only depending on what circumstance you're going through, but also because of where you have been and what you're able to relate to from personal experience.

As I mentioned earlier, there were some key reading materials I came across that spoke to me on the level I was on at the time. It helped me along my journey to emotional wellness, and helped me to reshape my self-image from the inside out. Of all the books I read and internet sites accessed, the key and most essential daily reading material was none other than the Holy Bible. I found that just one excerpt from the Bible a day, kept the depression demons away. During my quiet, vulnerable times, I would listen to inspirational books on CD or the religious radio station, to fill the silence on the car rides to and from work. I bombarded myself with constructive messages to help me drown out the noisy clutter of negative thought inside my head. It's very hard to beat away negative thoughts, but, when you really let go of your pain, these thoughts will either go away or you learn to see the lack of truth in them.

For me, the most significant change toward wellness, occurred when I finally found the courage to allow myself to feel the pain. Yes, that is what I said. When I tried to hide from the pain, it enveloped me. I had to look at it directly, and face why the hurt actually hurt, before I could ever learn how to work through it. Yes, this is difficult. Yes, at times you'd rather just hide. But hiding is completely ineffective; it will get you either no results, or unhealthy results. Some say if you hang in there, the answer is often just around the corner, but you can only get around the corner when you make the decision that you are ready to travel the road. You may have to stretch your inner-self in what feels like, unnatural ways. And did I say, yes, this hurts. Pain and self-growth go hand in hand. Out of one comes the other. I found out that the only way to conquer what was making me so unhappy about my situation was to look at it in the face, and figure out what I was most unhappy about. I asked myself what I really feared, where my bad feelings stemmed from, and what I thought this whole situation symbolized to me and about me.

When My Well Ran Dry

There was a time when I looked at myself and all I could see was a bag of negative energy. I literally hated myself and was angry that this had become my story. I walked around with a constant nagging headache, and lived in a continuously frustrated and sleep-deprived state. I felt completely and utterly unlovable. If my husband didn't love me, then who would? For a while, I could only come up with one heartrending reply, "no one". There was hardly anything good left within me. I felt completely empty. I had to find out why I felt this way about myself. I felt ashamed, unclean and unlovable. Like a leper, I found myself hiding in the shadows of my own life. What was this really all about after all? I'd always been a fighter. I fought long and hard to establish myself in so many other ways. I worked my way up from nothing into an extremely competitive career, and was well respected in my field. Why was this thing tripping me up so badly and completely distorting my view about the meaning of my entire life to this point?

I knew something had to change. I was ashamed to be thinking so little of myself. I was in my late thirties at the time, and could not bear the thought of wasting my life away, in this state. The very thought made me even more weary. In this state, I was destroying myself, and the only way to turn life around was to get rid of all the ugly images I had of myself and what I thought of my own worth to society. It took me yet another year to come up with a different reply to the question, "if my husband doesn't love me, then who will?" Finally I got up the nerve to reply...well, "me", of course! I had dig deep to find a reason to love myself again. Do you know how hard it is to dig deep into yourself? It's a figurative digging so at first, it is difficult to conceptualize. Sometimes it would take me two to three days to find any signs of inherent goodness within me. Loving myself, and forgiving myself for behavior in the past was another one of the most difficult things I've ever had to do in my life. It was harder than the very predicament that brought me here in the first place. My insides were like a bunch of raw nerve endings with loose wires of unaddressed issues that dated all the way back to being sexually molested at age four, up through the many bullies encountered through childhood and teenage years. It's only now I see that I had a very unhealthy idea of who I could trust, what I deserved, and what love was supposed to be like. I didn't ever think that being hurt by a friend, betrayed within my own family, teased or bullied in my youth had anything with who I am today. But all of these encounters helped to shape who I am today. So many of these encounters resulted in the branded messages: "you are unworthy on your own", "you need for other people to tell you that you are special" and "no one will really like the real you so just be who they seem to want".

I don't know exactly when, but eventually, a light bulb turned on finally making me realize that I'd fashioned my adult life around these subliminal messages. As a result of being on guard, I operated from a place of being fight-ready and pushing people away, but at the same time fearing abandonment. This paradox limited my ability to give freely as I was emotionally confused about how to interact with most people. It was not until I sifted through all of these circumstances that had me living like a caged animal from the wild, that I found a small glimmer of the real me who was buried under thirty-five years of rubble. I hardly recognized her. The person I found under the rubble, was a four year old little girl who was sexually and emotionally violated, and betrayed. A little girl who became confused about what it meant to be loved, feel special, and important. I met that little girl where she was, and slowly walked her through the circumstances of her life that made her develop defense mechanisms for emotional protection. Together, we slowly learned to understand these defense mechanisms. As I took her sweet little hand through the twists and turns of her life, she grew stronger. She eventually grew up to meet me in present day. When she caught up to me, together we understood why things happened the way they did, and why we made the choices that we did. Together, we gathered up all the loose wires of painful memories, and carefully rolled them into a neat little ball in the corner of our mind. That is when I fully accepted the presence of that little girl in me. It was not until then, that I realized I had the power to love the person inside—the me, inside of me. I spent my whole life trying to bring love in from an external source, even my husband. I never realized the love that I was seeking was really always mine to give. I just didn't know it. I had to go find the little girl in me, and love her through the stages it took for her to grow into womanhood. If only I'd known the jewel that always shimmered within, maybe I would have managed my life differently. Now I see more. Now I know better. The lightning bolt I thought was going to wake my husband up, struck me instead.

Acceptance

Chapter Eight:
You want a *what?*

*I*f I could make sound effects, I would end the title of this chapter with another flash of lightning and a *dah dah dah dant*. I finally realized that one day, I may very well be divorced. By the grace of God, I found the courage to step outside of my overly emotional state, and try to tackle my circumstance from a semi-objectional point of view. I decided to analyze why divorces happen, what went wrong in my own relationship, and why this divorce thing (which had now become it's own entity...the new beast in my life) was so personally frightening for me.

I think divorce as *a solution to* marital problems is an oxymoron. It is way too easily accepted in this country. You always hear that the divorce rate in America is 50 percent. That means one in every two marriages end in divorce! Well, I often wondered where these statistics came from.

CNN most recently reported that divorce rates are falling; however, other sources contradict this claim. The Center for Disease Control reports a marriage rate of 6.8 per 1,000 population, and the divorce rate as 3.4 per 1,000 population, compiling data from the "Births, Marriages, Divorces, and Deaths:

Provisional Data for 2009.[3]" Divorce.com ranks the world divorce rates as follows:

Worldwide Divorce Statistics
Worldwide Divorce Rates—Top 20
Countries with Highest Divorce Rates per Capita

1. Belarus 68%
2. Russian Federation 65%
3. Sweden 64%
4. Latvia 63%
5. Ukraine 63%
6. Czech Republic 61%
7. Belgium 56%
8. Finland 56%
9. Lithuania 55%
10. United Kingdom 53%
11. Moldova 52%
12. United States 49%
13. Hungary 46%
14. Canada 45%
15. Norway 43%
16. France 43%
17. Germany 41%
18. Netherlands 41%
19. Switzerland 40%
20. Iceland 39%
21. Kazakhstan 39%

On a world scale of top 20 countries with the highest divorce rates, the US fell at number 12 when this book was written.[3] Compiling the data available, I think analysis of the divorce rate is multifactorial. Couples who wait to marry later in life, when more financially stable, may have higher likelihood of success. Higher education, religion, and children all are major factors in marital success. Broken down by age group, it appears as though marriages between the ages of twenty to thirty are the highest risk group, having a 20 to 40 percent chance of divorce, where second and third marriages have a markedly high failure rate of 60 to 73 percent, respectively, as per Jennifer Baker of the Forest Institute of Professional Psychology in Springfield, Missouri. In 2011, Mexico City proposed a negotiable marriage license where you can sign up for a minimum of two years, an interesting but also slightly ludicrous alternative, in my opinion. What has happened to our values? I'm tempted to write President Barack Obama and ask that he declare the divorce rate in this country a state of national crisis. Someone needs to help us figure out what we're doing wrong. I don't even get excited anymore when people tell me they're getting married. I immediately think, *Do they know what they're doing? Who's helping them?* Why is it that a couple is just as likely to divorce as stay married? Is it a coin toss? Heads or tails, it's all the same odds? In subsequent marriages, the gap widens…unfortunately, in favor of divorce. Just walk through a grocery store and you're bombarded with tabloids reading: HE CHEATED! THE HONEYMOON IS OVER; THE $250-MILLION DIVORCE. It's nauseating how people are drawn in to hear the "juicy dirt" of what happened. How many would pick up a magazine of an old couple with grandchildren that said, WE HAVE A REGULAR LIFE AND STILL LOVE AND CARE FOR EACH OTHER. Not much flash or pizzazz there. In fact, some may find it actually boring.

Anyone who's gone through a painful divorce can probably admit somewhere that the pain of the process is damn near unbearable. So, even the people poked fun at in the tabloids have pain too, and worse, they have to share it with millions of strangers. Can their children walk through a grocery store or a magazine stand confidently with their friends? My heart goes out to them.

Hollywood has trivialized divorce, and tabloids exploit other people's pain. There's even a situational comedy on television entitled, *Happily Divorced*. The reality is that divorce is not happy or pretty? I don't see how suffering through this grueling, hurtful process is a better alternative than trying to see the other person's point of view and working things out. I bet if both parties in a divorce would mature a little bit and learn to let go of whatever they were angry about in the first place, divorce lawyers would have a lot less material to prey on.

Chapter Nine:

What I've Come to Learn about Marriage, Divorce, and Human Relationships in General

*I*t wasn't until my relationship with my husband fell completely apart, that I started spending so much time thinking about marriage and divorce. I first had to accept that this was my new reality. Acceptance of my situation came in waves and stages. For me this was an oscillating cycle with a wide spectrum of emotions. I analyzed, over-analyzed, and frequently relapsed back into states of extreme depression and anger. I found out things about myself during this time, that I did not know. I found out, that unbeknownst to me, much of my personal identity was married to the idea of being married. If I had to give up my "married woman" label, I couldn't figure out how to define myself. I felt like being "just me" wasn't enough. Just being by myself felt incomplete, like an unfinished story and surely not an end goal. This is what society and my upbringing did to me; encouraged me to believe that without a husband, I fell short. What an insult to women in general; a message that we are not enough. What does a message like this mean to a woman who chooses not to marry, or who wants to marry, but has not found the right mate? What does a message like this mean to little girls? A man by himself is a free spirit, or stud bachelor that can't be pinned down. A woman by herself is considered either an undesirable old maid that no one wants, or a frigid "I don't need a man" career driven bitch. Is this fair?

I openly confess that I felt like having the title of "married woman", secretly gave me some type of subliminal validity, an "acceptable" place in society, if you will. I belonged to a special group of those who had been claimed by another, wearing a band around a finger that says to the world,

I'm someone's top choice. But Jesus named the 2 greatest commandments; neither of them being that the goal of life is to have 2.5 children, and a dog. Man made that up, not God. I learned that my approach to marriage was all wrong, and the unhappiness that was within me was because what I expected just "being married", would do for me, is what I really should have been able to do for myself. It was me who should have declared myself acceptable.... on my own without a title or label...just because of my own personal qualities and why God sent me here in human form. If I'd embraced this at age 20, I may have been more selective about who I allowed in my life. Maybe. No way to know for sure.

I can't say that I understand the reasons behind all divorces. I doubt there's any simple answer to the question as to why do so many people go for the divorce option so frequently. There are situations of physical, emotional, or illicit substance-related abuse in which establishing a permanent distance is the healthiest and safest option for all involved. This is a unique subset of marital grievance that should be handled with the professional care and counseling it warrants. But what about all the cases that fall under the catchall basket heading of "irreconcilable differences"? Well, my theories about those are as follows:

In general, we are a self-centered society. People, myself included, rush into marriage without taking into consideration the complexity of this type of bond and the level of patience and compromise it will require over a wide spectrum of situations, events, and circumstances. I can't really comment on why there are high rates of divorce in other countries, but at least in America, I think we tend to become uncomfortable if we can't receive instant gratification. Whatever doesn't work is simply thrown away...even people. We tend to like our lives with high-speed access—Burger-Kinged or microwaved—which is a flaw for many Americans. If you spend time living in another country—not as a tourist but really live there—you may find that things don't work as quickly in other countries, and people are used to having to be more patient. Tourists are catered to, and given an easy lifestyle, so it really doesn't count when you go somewhere on vacation. If you try working in another country (Canada doesn't count), having an apartment, getting your utilities turned on, doing laundry, or grocery shopping, you may be quite frustrated that things are not quite as at your fingertips as they are here at home. Many people in this country lack the patience and the ability to put themselves in another person's shoes and view life from their perspective, giving the other person the benefit of the doubt or learning to speak their unspoken language. In the Dalai Lama's, *Little Book of Wisdom*[4], he describes that divine grace can be achieved with a little human to human empathy. His advice could likely bring harmony to any relationship, romantic or not. It is to our detriment how frequently we are unwilling to see the world from the other person's perspective.

We would do good to practice daily the "Love thy neighbor" rule, which is often the most difficult commandment to honor. Why we can't get along is an ongoing dilemma. It seems as though many of us humans *want* boundaries and *lines of distinction*. Why? These lines only separate us and pit us one against the other. Man against woman, human against human. Who ever really wins those battles? Whenever it gets hard for me to love another, I force myself to either see the good or see the pain inside that person. I remind myself that I show my love for God when I embrace the similarities I have with others, and respect the differences. You can find some kind of love for just about anyone this way.

Men and women appear to be able to work together in collegial harmony, and in some professions, consult with each other as near equals. (I say *near* because I'm not naïve enough to think that the good ol' boys don't exist anymore or, at the top of every ceiling, doesn't remain a little bit of glass). I work in a male-dominated profession; however, my male colleagues respect me, consult with me, and value my judgment and decision-making on a regular basis. When I'm at work, I do get a sense that I am the commander of a ship with a cargo of fragile human lives that require careful nurturing. I use a treatment plan grounded in evidence-based science, am an advocate for every patient, and have become good at complex problem solving. It appears as though I was not successful at applying the right type of problem solving skills at home or in my relationship with my husband. I didn't know how. I never learned that.

There was a point in my career, the busiest point, when my husband started getting very particular about housework. I thought, *what is it all of a sudden with the spotless house thing?* He never had these issues before? Granted our family was growing, so there were a lot more people and a lot more laundry. Surely I wasn't expected to manage the growing mess in our home, and keep up with my new career demands all at the same time. Was I? If not me, then who was supposed to do this work? I never came up with a feasible answer so I spit shined what was visible, swept the rest under the rug, so to speak, and carried on. I've heard that men want to come home to a castle. I was always strongly against marrying that type of man. I always wanted a career *and* equal partner. Maybe I was naïve, but I didn't think it was too much to want someone who would never expect me to do something that they wouldn't do themselves. The first man I was engaged to (at the way too early tender age of 21), looked at me when I was cleaning his grandmother's kitchen, no less, and said to me, "You know what I don't like about you? You don't get behind things." Excuse me? Come again? He found a dishrag in his face and ultimately a returned engagement ring in his hand. That's what I call a red flag! I did not marry him. I was too amazed at The nerve he could muster. And there were other things that just told me "no". I don't understand the whole man castle argument. We all remember what slob holes they lived in before marriage or in college. Mess didn't bother them then. Now, all of a sudden, they've converted to neat freaks; that is, as long as someone else is doing the cleaning. It's all so confusing. Do y'all just say you want a career woman, but secretly want a housewife from 1950 who holds a bachelor's degree from the charm school of female etiquette? I don't know. What I know is that I appreciate the many talents I *do* have, and admittedly none of them involve being a master homemaker. So all I can do is just shrug my shoulders as if to say *what am I gonna do, it's just not my forte?* I'm not a slob, I have an outside-of-the home full-time job, and I certainly don't want be accountable to a white glove inspection in my own home. I just don't think that's a fair fight. That's just how I see it.

Something Rick Johnson said in his book, *Becoming Your Spouse's Better Half*[5], struck me. He says that men put everything in little categories or compartments. Each compartment can, apparently, only be dealt with one at a time. I find that to be amazing. I do get that men may not interconnect complicated things the way that women do. It apparently doesn't make sense to them. So, wow, I knew they spoke a different language, and are from Mars and all, but can we really relate their strange behavior to concrete thinking and little unrelated compartments in their brains that are not allowed to touch each other? It makes me think of the little toddler plates with dividers that separate the peas from the carrots. I somehow think I've heard this same analogy somewhere else before. It may have been in *Men Are from Mars, Women Are from Venus*[6] by John Gray. There must be something to it. What puzzles me is that my colleagues deal with and interrelate complicated concepts all day long, but I guess they can do that at work because all work goes in the work compartment, and maybe the problem solving aspect gives a bit of a thrill. At work, they may more or less have specific questions to answer, that are easier to address than abstract "feelings" and "emotions".

It is commonly accepted that women are much more complex than men. In my opinion, I think we are more in tune with the inner workings of relationships as we are more detail oriented, nurturing, and emotionally adaptable. In having these gifts, women are often handed a unique task; that is, to make sure that all are tucked in and content before she rests. Children, bedtime stories, lullabies, and lots of hugs and kisses provide a reliable and mutually satisfying routine. Making a man feel content can be more complicated, and it apparently needs to change based on his mood at a given time. Women who have been married a long time are pros at making their men feel tucked, in a natural and loving way. I personally never mastered this and in retrospect, can see how I held back on being an openly loving partner. I was just too busy. I too, held on to resentments from old disagreements, and was too wrapped up in the busy routine of life to really deal with those resentments. Of course, I never in a million years would think this could be an absolute recipe for divorce. Not after so much time had been invested. Whatever happened to loyalty? Either one of us, could have set the other down to discuss our plight, and propose a workable solution. Did we really have to just tear our family apart? The experience, however, did echo to me how fragile human relationships can be, and the thoughtfulness that is required to maintain the health of such relationships. I guess I was naïve.

From the outside, the contemporary woman may look at a conventional wife as though they were primitive. On the contrary, I think conventional wives have found that by putting in just a little bit of strategically placed effort and thoughtfulness, they ultimately get everything they want out of their man. Keep in mind that this is not done manipulatively. I think it's a direct effect of the love they give and the way in which they give it, tailored to the specific needs of their mate—just as you would to your child in a way. It would have certainly come in handy if more women who have mastered wifery would share with the rest of us the tricks of the trade. It's not just luck. There is an art to it. Male-female relationships have been going on long enough that we really should be better at this. I think, deep down inside and with a little extra effort, we all can figure out how to do it. For example, a mother knows that with children, it is clear that they are all slightly different with slightly different needs. You give to them according to their needs, but it takes time and patience to learn how to make it "just right" for each individual child so they will receive maximum benefit from what you have to give. Willingly, and out of love, we try to help strengthen them wherever they are vulnerable. No matter who is on the receiving end, whether it be spouse, child, friend, or stranger, the act of giving becomes a rich exchange when the gift falls in line with what the giver naturally enjoys giving. If, however, you feel as though someone is trying to "take" something from you that you don't want to give, you may become emotionally defensive, frustrated, and giving will be difficult.

If I were to give advice to all the daughters of the earth, it would be this: A woman should not get married without knowing herself first and what she is willing or emotionally ready to give. She can then draw a more authentic line designating what is acceptable and unacceptable in her life. I think that is when you are in the best position to define what type of person would be your most suitable long-term companion for all the ups and downs life may bring. Much of this advice could go to both parties, but I focus on the woman since traditionally we are asked to be married, and therefore have the power to choose "yes" or "no" for the answer. So don't answer "yes", until you either know what you are doing, or have a "go to" place to get the answer. At first, you may have to work hard, but ultimately, it's about working smart...like so many other things in life. Women do this so well. We're supreme at pulling many pieces together, and making them all work. We tend to find a way to get the job done.

Marriage may possibly be the most challenging of all human relationships because it is so difficult to have someone else's best interest at heart all the time. My criteria were: cute, ambitious, bread-winner, wants kids, no cheater tendencies. This is not enough—lacks depth. We all come into these relationships with years of personal historical baggage that manifest over time. In that, each one of us is somewhat of an enigma that unfolds in layers over time and under different circumstances. I personally never really understood that self-sacrifice and giving are mainstays of marriage. I thought more of what I would get out of a marriage more than what I needed to put into it. All of this can be taught. All of this can be learned. We can do this, if we learn the rules. We can do anything, if we make it an act of love for our families. This is our collective strength my sisters.

There may be some truth to the old jingle...I can bring home the bacon, fry it up in a pan, and never ever let you forget you're a man.... 'cause I'm a woman....

As you can see, I'm very pro-woman, but that doesn't equate to being anti-man. All fun aside, I don't want to appear like I think the responsibility of a marriage going well lies solely on the shoulders of the female; nor do they fall on the male for that matter. Either party, however, has the power to shift things to a favorable or unfavorable outcome depending on the individual responses to circumstance. Marriage truly is a "special" kind of partnership. What I've come to learn is that things may not always be cut straight down the middle on a daily, weekly, or even monthly basis. The whole, "marriage should be 50/50 argument" is a bunch of bologna. This is an imprecise statistic that's irresponsibly and passively thrown out there even by people who have never been married. It is impossible to assign a numerical value that will accurately account for all the complexities of life, for everyone's life. The fraction of input from either party in a relationship fluctuates and teeter-totters depending on life's demands. In a good marriage, I believe things become mutually complimentary with time; where one party is strong, the other can be a little weaker, and vice versa. This is an observation that can be noted when looking back retrospectively at a multitude of scenarios you've faced as a couple over a period of time. Real-time scorekeeping is the unhealthy birthplace for grudge and resentment. So many of my friends, who have had failing relationships, tend to lay blame on the other party. It's always his fault or her fault. I've heard formal discussions on relationships with a central focus on how the woman in the story did wrong and didn't support her man, with inappropriate justification for reckless decision making as a response. I don't understand this reasoning. Does one wrong justify another? It may feel like a temporary, stand your ground type of win but ultimately leaves everyone just feeling either hurt or angry (which is really just hurt under disguise).

Maybe pointing fingers, particularly at the woman, goes back to the Garden of Eden described in the Bible's book of Genesis. Yes, we all know that Eve gave Adam the forbidden fruit, but he ate it, didn't he? She didn't hold him down, whip him, and shove pieces down his throat against his will. The reality is both parties were held accountable for their choices. One is not guiltier than the other. History tells us that pointing fingers really gets us nowhere.

My story is from one female's perspective, after my own personal experience. I'm just a regular person like everyone else. Maybe men should seek relationship advice from male relationships experts. I think Rick Johnson does a very good job of giving both sides of the story in *Becoming Your Spouse's Better Half.* He highlights specific things men can do to support and bring out the best in their women.

As a woman, I can tell you a little secret about us. A woman likes to feel like she is important to her man, like she and what she wants really matters to him. Some like to be showered with expensive material gifts and flowers. Some like gifts all the time; some like them only on occasion or sporadically. Some women actually don't care much at all about material gifts, contrary to popular belief, but would prefer to be given your undivided attention intermittently, a kind gesture, an occasional compliment, a walk in the park holding hands, or just to be given a little "she" time every now and then, to unwind. Most of these acts can be completed in thirty minutes or less, which is not much to ask of you on any given day. I think there is an unfortunate misconception that most women want a man who makes a lot of money—providing her with material things, monumental gifts, and taking her to expensive places—gold-diggers who will always want and expect more. That is an evil lie that has been passed down through generations and represents a very small subset of women. With many of us, simple little everyday things go a very long way. If men pay a little attention and give to a woman according to her particular needs and desires, you would be pleasantly surprised with the abundance of gratitude very small acts of consideration can bring you—a large return on a small investment of yourself, your patience, and your time.

A woman who feels loved, acts loving-ly. You all know how to make your woman feel special. You know what she likes and doesn't like. Didn't you do all those little special things when you first courted your sweetheart? Why would you stop doing these things when you get married? I hardly think you would have won her hand in the first place if you spent all of your time farting on her couch and rubbing your belly. Maybe your wife is disgruntled because you don't do the things you used to do. If you don't want to put forth the effort even for thirty minutes at a time, do the girl a favor and don't marry her or anyone else until you're ready to commit. Just politely tell her what your limitations are so she can move on if she desires. In the interim, please maintain control of where your sperm lands. The presence of children makes everything more complicated. At any point, either party can step outside of a situation and make a mature decision about what needs to happen to heal a relationship or keep it healthy. We don't always do it that way, but we definitely are able to.

So if your marriage falls apart, is it really going to matter who said this or who didn't say that, who did too much of this or who didn't do enough of that? What will you win? There's no prize in that. I don't even remember what my husband and I were fighting about so often or why. None of it really matters when I think of how I felt when he was no longer around. Someone needed to be the mature one. As far as how you need to interact with each other, I find that if you're really kind to the one you love, unless something is mentally wrong with them or they have a mind altering addiction, they tend to want to be kind in return.

Chapter Ten:
Did You Choose Your Mate Well? Did I?

 or women, being a supreme multi-tasker may be a God-given gift. Multi-tasking is a bit of a misnomer since you really can only devote focus to one thing at a time. Women do, however, seem to have a knack for keeping multiple responsibilities and schedules floating around in our heads and can retrieve several facts, at any given time, with ease. This retrievable data package of details most definitely serves a purpose for the welfare of the family unit. I joke with my friends that after God made Adam, he realized that this dude was going to need some help…and then came Eve. No offense to the men out there, but I like to think of females as the perfected model of the human prototype. Think of all the things we are designed to do. We are complex beings. All of humanity is born of our womb. Not only are we built to sustain life within us, but we can also nourish it once it's born of us. The cycle upon which our womb sheds it's lining links us to the universe and to each other, rebuilding itself monthly in concordance with the gravitational pull of the moon and the tides of the oceans. We are all that is feminine, soft, and beautiful. We are God's masterpiece, created to nurture and sustain the human species. Ladies, this is not something we should flaunt but absolutely something all of us should treasure. I think the song *I'm Every Woman* by Whitney Houston, should be the female world anthem and Maya Angelou's *Phenomenal Woman*, our signature poem. May God rest their beautiful souls. Wear this information like a badge of quiet honor signifying feminine strength.

It's difficult for men to do things that come quite naturally to us; some things they just can't do at all. When I ran into trouble with my husband, I began to ask myself, *How could I have chosen someone who would do this to me? How could I pick someone who wouldn't think I was worth fighting for and sticking it out with?* I don't know all the reasons yet why this happened in my marriage, but if I had to advise the yet unmarried (and I just can't say it enough): take time to choose your life mate. Before putting anyone in your life, your top priority project should be working on yourself. When you learn to look into the depth of your own soul, you can learn to see the soul of others.

In college, I remember using a logo that read the words "*Know Thyself*". At the time, I thought it was catchy, but did not understand the depth inside of these two words. As I look back I always wish that I'd really listened to those words I used so casually. On my own personal journey, I really found out what made me tick and why. I learned where my trigger spots were for anger, resentment, and hurt. In my case, these places stemmed from childhood demons and resulted in development of defense mechanisms. Childhood molestation is unfortunately common. Although no one can erase their past, I found it important to understand how events of my own childhood may have impacted the way I felt about myself growing up, and influenced decisions that I may not have made, had the events never occurred. When my emotional "sore" spots were rubbed in the wrong way, hostile outbursts would almost always follow. I looked at myself and realized what limited insight I used to understand my own emotions in *many* interpersonal encounters. The lack of control I had over myself, caused me unhappiness in several areas of my life and eventually wore through the thin places in my marriage.

If you have hang-ups from your past that prevent you to love freely, you would do best to figure out how they contribute to glitches in your personality. Only through dissecting your individual hang-ups will you understand why your hang-ups formed. As I said, it takes time to ask yourself, "What is the underlying issue that is the driving force behind my hang-ups?" Why do I react to certain things the way I do? What does that reaction stem from? Some unresolved issues maybe? You may have to ask yourself the question several different ways to really get to the core of the problem, why it formed, what you think it meant at the time it was formed, and what you think it means about you now. I pulled apart each one of my hang-ups and looked at them one by one. This journey of introspect took me deep into my childhood and forced me to be honest with myself about some very unpleasant memories. The reward after each dissection, however, was an acceptance of the raw me, the one inside who was trying to protect herself. There is deep reward that comes out of traveling to the inner space of who you are, without the mask you put on in front of society. Initially this is tough, because you may find that you're ashamed of past behavior, choices, and the truth of the intention behind those choices. What you find in the confines of your memory may even scare you. Forgive yourself for not knowing better at the time. Forgive yourself for being afraid. It's ok. Everyone has this turmoil going on inside, even your spouse or whoever you are dealing with. Forgiving yourself for not being perfect gives you the freedom to really love yourself, and opens you up to loving the core pieces of other people. It helps you to *forgive* other people for also, not knowing any better. This advice is not only helpful for marriages, but all human relationships.

So if I can add to "*Know Thyself*", I would also say, "*Love Thyself—Honor Thyself*". If you don't, there will be serious problems, so you must work on this first and foremost. Remember you are your own precious jewel on the inside, and deserve top choice. Somewhere in my formative years, I was somehow brainwashed into thinking that men were a rare commodity; a prize to win. I don't think I'm alone in this. Some of us have lowered our standards to be with them. I finally figured out that *we* are the prize. As Eve was to Adam, *we* are the gift. We are a masterpiece. If all women agreed to raise our standards, men would rise to the occasion and treat us differently as a whole. Those who know their true strength never have to broadcast, become punitive or unladylike. There is just a certain standard you need to have about yourself and who you allow to be inside of your intimate spaces. Tease through your options for companionship with great effort and insight. It's not like picking a pair of shoes. (Although, if they were really nice heels that you needed to walk around in every day, all day long. I know you would put those babies to the test of several different acrobatic scenarios to ensure they were up for the challenge of toting your tootsies in style, grace, and with as much comfort as could possibly be expected). If you underestimate the durability and fit of a pair shoes, you can always just stick them in the back of your closet; you can't do that with a man. You may get locked up.

If you live in a culture where you get to decide whether or not you want a mate (and it's really ok if you don't want to), the first step is to start with good working material. First off, are you good working material? Do you have unresolved issues? Having a mate won't fix this, it won't "complete" you. Only you can mend your innermost wounds. Do that first before you bring someone else into the picture. Then you can look at your prospects objectively. I caution you that there's only so much you can do with a lifelong playboy, a crackhead, or a wife-beater. Face the reality that some people are just hazardous to your health. So, for goodness sake be picky. It may take you a little longer to link up with an ideal mate, but it will save you a lot of heartbreak in the end. Learn what it really takes to be happy. You will find that happiness is not in a label, title, thing, or another person. No one thing or person in your outer world should hold this power. What if you give all that power to that thing or person, and something happens to that thing or person? Physical things get destroyed, people can leave your life, die, or get run over by a bus. Then where will you be?....lost! Learn what you like and dislike, what you are about and what you stand for, then decide who has qualities that are worthy of *you*. I would have rather waited until age forty to marry and have a blissful thirty plus years with my husband than marry at twenty-three before either of us knew ourselves, what we wanted, or why we wanted it. Don't let lies society feeds you about old-maidship or ticking-bio-logical-clock trick you into making a hasty and unwise decision. Remember, half of Americans who marry may divorce, so they obviously don't have all the right answers either. Take advice from people who actually know what they're doing. Learn about your own capacity to love, as well as your limitations. If you've never been married or thinking of remarrying, you must read, *Whom Not to Marry—Time-Tested Advice from a Higher Authority.*[7] It's written by a Catholic priest, Father Pat Connor, who spent years counseling married couples and saw plenty of red flags in his day. He's hilarious, but in all seriousness, if women took complete ownership of keeping a healthy self-esteem and honoring it at all cost, we would be better at sifting through the foolishness early and would choose better mates.

You have to really dig down to define your own purpose and potential. Learn what it really takes to make yourself happy. Newsflash: it is NOT going to be simply just having a mate. It's got to be something that's all about YOU and why YOU were put on the earth in the first place. The concept is abstract, and requires you to stretch your way of thinking. Our world today doesn't teach us to think with self-depth. We are drunk with superficial goals, superficial living, and short-sighted thinking. You can do better than this. To rise above your prior conditioning requires a deliberate act of your will. When you want change bad enough, you will change. Exert the effort and you can find the answers to life's hardest questions. Ultimately, you will find that you are happiest when you can be yourself and not feel compelled to wear a fake mask for someone else's approval or acceptance. We all wear some kind of mask out in public. Find out what his life purpose is, and what he's really like without the mask he's fashioned for society. How have his life experiences jaded his personality, and to what extent? When you both get bogged down with the details with life, that loving feeling wears off, waxes and wanes. Pressures of regular daily living, children, careers, and running a household build. The mask will eventually come off, and what remains is the raw you. It's best if you know who that fundamental person is and how they (and you) behave under pressure or you may one day wake up next to *two* total strangers.

Try not to lose sight of what's really important in life. Don't let minutia wreck your relationships. If your man thinks a clean house is essential and you don't want to or are just too busy to do it, find a creative way to make extra money and pay someone else to do whatever you don't want to do yourself. Make sure you don't dig into the household pot. Men can get funny about money, especially in this economy. This is my opinion, but you may not want to just pool all of the money into one pot and try to share it. I was naïve enough in my marriage to think we could share everything…including money. Wrong! When my husband left, he took his money with him, and I found myself short of funds. Instead of the previous image of the woman who really "had it going on," I abruptly felt more like a clumsy ballerina in toe shoes trying to balance on a financial tightrope. Initially, I was terrible at balancing the money I had to work with. When I realized that many people learn to do more with less, I decided to tighten my belt, suck in my gut, and regain poise. I actually wished that I'd spent more time as a single woman learning how to do these things on my own, before joining dysfunction with malfunction in a marriage, being the know-it-all I was in my twenties, I thought I could figure anything out. Now with five mouths to feed, a new dog, and a limited budget, I had to make a drastic change to my spending habits. I decided to just stop using my debit card, gave myself a weekly cash-only allowance, and, inspired by the extreme couponing reality TV show, I got to clipping. I wish I'd learned the art of household budgeting when my husband was at home. We would have had fewer arguments about money …one less thing. Toward the end, I was just so overwhelmed with how many things were slipping through my fingers, I didn't have the wherewithall to find practical solutions to all the little things that seemed to be going wrong. It all just spiraled out of control so quickly, and I didn't know how to stop it.

Ladies, I would advise having a rainy day pot that keeps you both happy in knowing that your future is secure. But you can keep your own stash of cash…call it your miscellaneous account from which you can do whatever you want with. A great book to read is *Secrets of the Millionaire Mind*[8] by T. Harv Eker for sound advice on how to manage money well. Tell him that you want to handle money responsibly and not risk the household funds on something like a Coach handbag. Many men appreciate a woman who is money conscious. If you find someone who doesn't care about squandering money, make a polite excuse and strongly consider getting away from *that* guy; your future may not be secure. You don't want a life filled with headache and the limitations that living with bad credit can bring.

As grown women, I'm now convinced that we need to handle this marriage thing in a smart and intelligent way like we handle everything else in life. We need to abandon the "Walt Disney World" brainwashing some of us were raised with. Fairy tales and puppy love is for little girls playing dress up and teenagers. Modern day sequels aside, Cinderella's story ended at the wedding. She never disclosed the details on how she kept her happily-ever-after… happy forever after. So, do your research before saying "I do." Make sure that you really do, and you really will. Spend less time fussing over the wedding as an event, and spend more time preparing yourself to be connected to another human being for a lifetime. I'm not saying that your marriage will then be perfect; life in general is a challenge. But I think many of us saw red flags before the wedding that only escalated and then spiraled out of control once we were married with children. Specifically, when children are a part of your story, you're more likely to feel trapped or apt to put up with things that would lead you straight to the door when you were not a parent. When you have children, you're also so exhausted with meeting their many needs. When exhausted, it's quite challenging to step outside of your everyday life and think of things in a level-headed non-emotional way. It's very difficult to problem solve in that state of mind.

So, from the start, know what you want and get all your ducks in a row, so that even when you're not at your full game, you still know how to communicate with him. Always stay two steps ahead of your man. When he comes into a room, you should shift your consciousness just a little and have a plan in mind to know how to handle whatever "box" he's speaking from. This all can be done with grace and intuition. And if you don't know what to say then just listen. By listening you may be able to figure out what his "main purpose" is, or what is really important to him. You'd be amazed how if you take the time to notice and be sensitive to a man's "purpose" you can find ways to help him achieve it or help assuage concerns he has about whatever it is he strives for. If you want to procreate, that's a whole 'nother level of commitment. Iron out the details ahead of time on who is going to do what. Don't just take it for granted that everything will just fall into place. Children bring in a stress factor that can be unbelievably difficult to overcome. Talk about expectations and sacrifices ahead of time, and along the way so that everyone, including you, can feel taken care of.

Whether you have children or not, your feelings toward your mate is something you always have the power to consciously change by focusing on the thing about him/her that you fell in love with in the first place. The moment your spouse's entrance to a room has absolutely no effect on you whatsoever, that's when life with him/her can be perceived as boring, ordinary, and unfulfilling. Do something about this quickly. Keep a subtle inner vibrance and an always caring spirit about you. Keep yourself emotionally healthy with reinforcements that have nothing to do with anyone else but you. In my own personal journey, I finally learned that water never comes from a dry well. When you learn how to fill yourself up from within, your internal well will overflow, you will be free to give, and your relationships will not become mundane. Try to practice loving him from a higher perspective. Think of him as God thinks of him, love him as God loves him. With a love like that, how can you go wrong. *'Blessed is he who comes in the name of the Lord.'* So bring it! In the words of Dr. Wayne Dyer, "If you change the way you look at things, then the things you look at will *change.*"[9]

**"Even after all this time the sun never says to the earth, 'You owe me'.
Look what happens with a love like that. It lights the whole world." – Hafiz**

Chapter Eleven:
Knowing Your Roots, Weaknesses, and Strengths

J've already alluded to the theory that my early childhood experiences may have set me on an initial path of destructive internal thinking. It's difficult to know how the absence of my father may have added to the insult. I was not raised with a father in the home. My parents divorced when I was five years old, and we moved from New York to California—2400 miles away from him. We grew up quite poor, financially. My mother gave us the gift of good values and a spirit of determination, none of which money can buy. We left him long before unlimited cell phone dialing and the internet. Long-distance calls were scarce, and visits were infrequent. After my parents divorced, I only saw my father on four separate occasions before I reached adulthood: a grand total of six times total in his lifetime. The last time I saw him, he was blind, on a ventilator, and three weeks away from death.

Since I took it so hard when my husband left, I've often wondered if male abandonment was another one of my unrecognized Achilles' heels, birthed in childhood experiences. Where my husband took me was somewhat an unchartered ground. I guess that unconsciously, I was always the one to jet when things got a little hot, to ensure that I was the dumpER and not the dumpEE, as one of my friends once put it. Call me old-fashioned and sentimental if you will, but pledging to spend your life with someone in marriage is much more special than your everyday run of the mill relationship. My husband caught me off guard as I was comfortable in my role as his wife and would never have even dreamed of leaving it. In addition, I never wanted to be divorced and have children who would grow up without a father as my siblings and I did. Once, a newly widowed woman told me that losing her husband was like losing her security blanket. I thought that was such a meaningful analogy. I listened to her story, and my heart wept for the ache I saw behind her eyes. I did not share my story because I didn't think she would see any similarity. Divorce is so commonplace that the average onlooker is desensitized to the psychological damage incurred by the ones going through this type of loss.

Even though I've been blessed with a successful career and am technically able to stand on my own two feet, having my husband with me provided me with a sense of security—a security that was now lost. I considered my husband to be my best friend through all of my adult life. In him, I confided everything. Knowing that he had my back and would be there to catch me if I fell *was* a safety net of comfort for me. It wasn't until he left that I realized what little confidence I had without his presence as a backup. I wanted to figure out how I had become so fearful. At what point in my life did I decide I needed to hide behind "someone" or "something"—anything that was acceptable? But what was *un*acceptable, exactly? And to whom? Who was I really trying to please?

Before this event, I always thought I was of strong character, but when my husband left, I crawled into a shell and became crippled with shame, worthlessness, and self-doubt. I didn't like what I'd become. I felt unattractive, unlovable, and embarrassed. I was pitiful; wrapping up so much of my own self-worth in the presence or absence of having my husband in my life. I'm not a psychiatrist, but I somehow think that the way I handled my husband's behavior has something to do with the absence of my father. I essentially felt unprotected. Even if you're not aware of it, unaddressed father-daughter relationship issues may surface their ugly head at inopportune moments when you're stressed, tired, and most vulnerable. Maybe it wasn't your father, but an emotionally unavailable mother. Maybe it was something else. Whatever hurt you back there in your memory banks, deal with this and understand what you're supposed to do with it before you take on a husband as they really are full-time jobs and need to be handled with a clear head. If you're a career woman who also wants to be married with children, be prepared to be able to have several full-time jobs even if you're not Jamaican.(I'm a child of Jamaican parents, so I can say that with a smile). In all reality, you may find that you have to simultaneously manage being partial breadwinner, household organizer, and, the most challenging part, being wife and mother. Juggle these roles like a skilled clown in a circus act while you figure out how to squeeze in some time for yourself, so that you remain emotionally healthy and not lose yourself. A woman who loses herself to all her many roles is easy prey for being very deeply scarred by life's erratic changes. I know because I am that woman.

Chapter Twelve:
Reality—Maneuvering through Midlife Ups and Downs

*A*round the fourth decade of a man's life, your marriage can become quite vulnerable. You must pay close attention. I think men must go through some type of male form of PMS, where they suddenly feel bloated, ugly, and crave things that are fast and sweet to assuage the pain of feeling like *they* don't measure up. In my husband's mid-forties, he seemed more impatient, less tolerant, and ready to abandon things that didn't go right. The thought never dawned on me that I could one day be on his list of things he'd let go of or abandon. Even if the changes are subtle, listen more than you speak, my friends. Be supportive even when you don't feel like it. It will pay off when his personal storm passes by. Be realistic in your thinking, however. It takes a very long time to earn she-stood-by-me-during-the-rough-time points with some men. They may be almost dead before they realize what you were there for. But you certainly don't want the consequences of not standing by them. It's the reason God made woman in the first place, right? Between the ages of forty to fifty, don't be surprised if your man becomes slightly odd and unpredictable. Recognize the signs of his midlife and fortify the foundation of your union so that it can sustain some pressure.

As women, we have all the right tools to make all of this work, but realistically, you need a game plan. Mastering the art of understanding your husband—reading his body language and figuring out what "compartment" he's acting out of or speaking from—I think, will teach you the secret of maneuvering through your marriage in a smart way, because love and la-la land from which fairy tales are made of don't last forever. I thought that my husband and I were so perfect for each other that we'd be immune to failure, and that nothing could ever possibly split us up. How arrogant and silly of me to not understand that no person or thing is immune to failure; conscious effort has to be put forth to maintain good working order in any relationship. Lust and good sex, even that initial loving feeling, bear no long-term sustenance. It's easy to get addicted to the euphoria of love. Is it realistic to think that you will always be euphoric about the one you love? Seems silly, but we expect it. When the euphoria is gone, we believe the love is gone too. Why can't we figure out that the reason you felt loved, is, in large part, because you behaved loving-*ly*. This is the egg that came before the chicken or however you want to look at it. When love matures, giving becomes more natural, and then the people doing the loving are more successful at weathering the peaks and valleys of life, because the default plan is to just "give more love and understanding". This is not intuitive, but it's worth figuring it out. Instinct just says, protect yourself from being harmed or slighted. You must know which relationship battles should actually be fought, and how. Be smart upfront to win in the end.

Make an informed decision about what you want. If you have a relationship that's worth something to you, you must put in the work to nourish it. Is any argument worth you permanently losing your mate? Do you want to win in the end or lose to a painful divorce? Splitting up children, chaotic visitation schedules, maladjusted teens or disoriented toddlers, dividing money, property, friends, family is no fun at all. I once met a blended family with three sets of kids—two sets from second marriages, one set from third marriage, and one from single parenthood—who juggled children back and forth every Wednesday, variable other weekdays, and every other weekend between four households. My word! I kept thinking, *How is that healthy?* Now I find myself in a similar boat, which brings to mind the lesson I learned about judgment.

Judgment can have a boomerang effect, so be careful who or what you criticize, as you may one day find yourself walking in those very same shoes. If you see something you don't like, pray that the other person finds strength to overcome that adversity. I never wanted to be a single mother. I felt like the title of "single mom" shouted naked and lacking, part of a whole if you will. I didn't want to be in that group. I didn't want to feel like half as good, or that I had half missing, or that my family was half of the standard. And I never wanted to be pitied. Like, "oh she's a 'single mother', let's give her a break". I didn't like that. I'm ashamed that I, myself, put this group in a special category. I abhorred being put into any category that had any type of sub-standard connotation. Here I had done the very thing I abhorred, snubbed my nose at someone else's plight (even my own mother's), one that had now become my own. Here in lies where one of my lessons would be. To not hold myself above or beneath any other. Deepak Chopra and the Dali Lama both speak of this principle of empathy for fellow man. These are the teachings of Jesus Christ. To see ourselves, in one another. It was not until well into my struggle I learned that everyone faces adversity in life, and this adversity can be the birthplace of strength. I can now see that the beauty of the "single mom" is that she has learned the lesson of resiliency and sheer grit to maneuver through life. In that lies great power. Why before this, had a been so blind? I once saw a breast cancer awareness shirt with the words, "Fight like a girl!"...Although I don't have breast cancer, when I saw these words I thought, *that actually sums up what single mother's do*. And so it goes that I now embrace being part of a new tribe of versatile women, and best of all, I've really learned how to fight like a girl;-)

I learned to never put myself above anyone else's struggle, as we can all find ourselves in each other's predicaments. There are no guarantees in life, one way or the other. Now I just try to use the stories of others as a learning experience about things that are in the realm of human possibility and capability. In the face of adversity, what would *you* have to fall back on? Is it something external to you or do you travel within yourself to find the answer? Maybe these questions can help you to figure out what you're made of; your true nature. What if when we looked at people, *all* we could see was their true nature? That would be an eye-opening experience, wouldn't it. What is your true nature? Are you proud of it?...Why? What is your mate's nature? Are you kind? Is he? What makes either of you happy? What makes you hurt? How have your life circumstances shaped the personality you project to the outer world? Do you understand your control over this? If you dig deep to find the answers to such questions, you can make better decisions about how you interact with everyone, including your mate. We have many resources around us to help us with relationships. You just have to realize that we all need help from the beginning, to prevent troubles, not only after the trouble has already arrived. By the time I consulted with all of the books I've read and internet websites, my marriage had already reached a critical low. I wish I had been forewarned and armed with some very basic advice from the git go.

If you are like me, you are an emotional and deeply feeling creature. It serves well for nurturing children, rescuing wounded birds, and taking in stray cats. Where would the world be without us? When you have your own feelings of sadness and self-doubt, work some of it out before bringing it to your husband. Men don't seem to handle emotional overload well or how critical we are of ourselves before we find our inner worth. I think it frankly confuses them, and their conclusions about our behavior are far from any conclusion your girlfriends would ever arrive at. So have a bubble bath, go out on a girls' night, and get most of it worked out in your own way before bringing it to him. I'm telling you, if you sob to your husband too many times, he'll start to think you're an unstable wreck, a drag to be around, and may even think you're weak...which, ladies, with all that we tackle on a daily basis, we know that couldn't be farther from the truth. Find a nurturing, supportive, and safe way to tend to your own emotional needs. Most times this needs to be independent of your spouse, but never shut your spouse out or emotionally withdraw. That may hurt their feelings. Learning how to care for yourself, and providing support for your intimate circle, takes practice.

Hope

Chapter Thirteen:
Back to the Bible.
Why the Good Book Is Really Quite Good

*I*n 2003, one of my patient's caretakers stopped me, looked me straight in the eye, and said to me, "You need to read your Bible. I don't know why, but God put it in my heart to tell you that." I felt exposed and ashamed. How did she know that at age thirty-two, I'd never read the Bible? Why did she think I needed to? Did I seem un-Godly? Hmmm, how very strange.

I intermittently thought of her words, but I did not actually pick up the Bible to read it seriously until 2008 when my husband dropped his bomb on me. At first, I didn't know how to read the Bible. I started with what I call Russian roulette Bible reading. I plopped open the book, and whatever page it opened to, I'd read there…naively thinking that divine intervention would magically lead me to the verses I needed to hear. It would take me years of fumbling around with that approach to finally learn *how* to read the Bible using some pointers I learned in adult confirmation class. A few years ago, I decided to re-do my confirmation as an adult with my teenage son. One of our confirmation packets advised that when you read a story in the Bible, imagine yourself as a character in that story, physically there in that time and space, to absorb the lesson of that story. Then take the lesson of that story and meditate on how it applies to your everyday life. Wow! What a difference that little piece of advice made for me. This practice also introduced me into the world of meditation and quiet self-reflection.

My priest advised that I start with the book of Acts to grasp what the apostles went through after they experienced the descent of the Holy Spirit upon them at Pentecost. For a while, I would read one chapter at a time every morning and meditate on the message and how I could apply it to

---

my day and my life in general. This small act made the difference between me having a lousy day and a very good one. I found that when I skipped my Bible reading, I felt like a wilted flower by the day's end. When I did it, I felt like I could take on many of the things that came my way. A little over a year before this, someone at work told me the very same thing. She said that if she always keeps her spiritual connection with God strong, everything else in her life falls into place. Something I heard one year prior, in a random conversation now became a key part of me climbing out of my real-time daily grief. This type of random, unexpected guidance is a little act of wonder that makes you think, "hmmm, isn't that funny how that worked out?". Signs of divine intervention are revealed to us all the time. We're often not even aware of the miracle at the time when it's given or how it will later come in handy. I think of it like Voldemort in Harry Potter, who put little pieces of himself into Horcruxes in which he would live on forever. Well, he got the idea from the Creator. First off, God put little bits of Himself inside of each of us called the Holy Spirit. This spirit rises up within you during times of stillness that make you feel close to God. If we're not aware enough to notice this presence, He has placed little angels that circle around us in our everyday lives, to love and protect us. Notice who your angels are. Some are seen, and I believe most are unseen... You must train yourself to look carefully for God's gifts that are surrounding you. It is very easy to be blind to them. These are the modern day miracles, the things that happen to you that can't be explained. I could not explain them but I knew there were little instances where I would feel alive and good inside, and saved from peril.

My whole life since my husband left has been surrounded by miracles and miracle workers. Doors have opened when I didn't even try to open them. Friends popped out of nowhere to help me in times of need, when I couldn't leave work in time to pick up my youngest children from afterschool care, or when I just needed someone to talk to. I remember one year the children and I had swine flu, and I was all alone with them. We all had fevers and could barely get out of bed. During the worst of it, one night, while lying in bed, I thought I saw a tall shadow outside by bedroom door. Thinking this was delirium, I just rolled over. The next morning, my refrigerator was full of variety of juices that my dear friend from across the street brought over, so that we could have plenty of liquids to drink. Then there was the time I didn't have enough money to pay for tuition, and it so happened that my mother, who, for seemingly no reason, asked to work extra shifts for about two months prior, was able to help me. And there was the babysitter from heaven who was referred to me by a random nice lady at the beauty parlor, just about two weeks prior to my taking on more clinical duty. Think about it, these things happen to all of us. Haven't you ever had an unexpected phone call from an old trusted friend when you felt like all your coworkers were out to get you, or the calm that suddenly quiets you have after you've gone through a rampage of violent tears, or when your five-year-old comes up behind you with a great big hug and says, "You're the best mommy ever...I love love you this (*arms opened wide*) much."

Fortunately, for me, God has not only surrounded me with angels, He has also somehow shielded my children through all of this. They really are the most loving and wonderful children anyone could ever ask for. It's as though God gave me enough strength to absorb all the hurt and leave them unscathed (or so I only hope). It truly amazes me to look at them and see what happy children they all are. You often hear how negatively affected children are by marital strife. My husband and I have kept most of our disagreements away from them to protect them. He is also very kind to them. He is interested and involved in their lives and has an uncanny ability to make them all feel very special. Initially this angered me. It was easy for me to think, "Oh, he's just overcompensating because he's guilty." Eventually I realized that no matter what drives my husband, my children would be maladjusted if he did not remain emotionally attached to them despite his physical absence from our home. I am now actually quite thankful for his desire to remain engaged in this way, as not all estranged husbands will do what he does. The way he remains engaged with them, and the way in which we love them, may very well be the reason why they seem so okay with everything as it currently stands. I always pray that we won't see some late effects in the children that we can't yet recognize now. They are a true blessing to us, and there really are not enough words to describe just how wonderful they are. The Christmas I started writing this book, was my first Christmas without them. That year, they pooled their money together and gave me a cross with the word FAITH in the middle. The rest reads as follows:

Trust in the Lord with all your heart;
Do not depend on your own understanding.
Seek His will in all you do, and HE will direct your paths...
...He rewards those who sincerely seek Him.
Proverbs 3:5-6, Hebrews 11:6.

After I read this message of faith given to me by, of all people, young children, my then six-year-old son looked up at me and said, "Put it by your bed, and you can read it every morning."And that's exactly what I did. Their second gift was a jewelry/music box, which on the outside reads:

"Children are like seeds in a Garden. A mother's love is like the warm sunlight that makes them grow and blossom".

When I opened it, the music didn't play. They were so upset, and after a few minutes of jiggling it and fidgeting with it, my oldest daughter said, "That's okay, we'll just sing you the song it played." On the count of three, they all sang in unison:

"Lean on me, when you're not strong, and i'll be your friend, I'll help you carry on. For it won't be long, 'till I'm gonna need somebody to lean on".

If that's not the most precious thing, then I don't know what is. They are the most thoughtful and loving children. I think the box malfunctioned just so I could hear them sing the song to me the first time, because about a week later, I opened it and the song played perfectly fine. I don't think any of these things are mere coincidences. God has graced my children with the gift of happiness. They are happy, when I'm happy, and show concern when I look not so happy. I don't want to seem like they are perfect or anything; they're kids and do regular kid-type things. But I find them to be particularly conscientious, and they really try to be good. I think it's because they don't want to disappoint me. Doing good will always benefit them, no matter the impetus, so I don't interfere with what motivates them. I just let them be, and they never cease to amaze me. I often wonder how on earth I've been so blessed with such loving children. I consider them a beautiful gift from heaven.

I know that the happiness I see in my children and all the things that really do just "miraculously work out" are all God's grace, blessings that come to us for seemingly no reason at all, out of nowhere at all. These are the things that strengthen the spirit within us and carry us through the rough times. I believe this is what the poem "Footprints in the Sand" is all about—God carries us through the rough times. I remember hearing older people say, "God is good all the time." I never knew, really, what that meant until I relied on Him to get me through every five-minute interval of a day.

The force of God always shows up. It is the same force behind my own heartbeat, my own breath. He is reliably and always there simultaneously keeping everything else around me, moving through cycles of life. I used to pray to God in heaven above, but sometimes felt as though I were calling on a distant relative. I really stumbled upon an eerie sense of oneness with God when one night during prayer, I turned by gaze inward, to look at the center of what made me, me. I found God here. This is the same way I found the little girl that was buried inside of me. As a matter of fact, the reason why the hurt little girl in me is so easy to love, is because God made that little girl. When I went back to the me that was, when I was pure and untainted, I realized that all these parts of me, persisted within me, cloaked under a loving robe of grace. When I realized this, I could then see how God was with that little girl through every step it took to grow her into her womanhood. I could see that He was always there in full force, even when she arrived at bad places in her life, including the one she was trying to get out of right now, just as foretold in the Footprints poem. It only goes to follow that I must love me, since I love her; as she is me and I am her. I hope that makes sense. Take a few minutes to think about this. For me it was an incredible revelation in how to love myself, no matter what. I don't know if you call this finding my inner child or what, but all I know is that I started wanting to be with this sacred place inside myself more and more. It started to feel like my safe zone—a place of contentment. I started to question, "what is that *feeling* that is in there that is so hard to describe?...Is it my soul?...Is it my spirit? What's the difference between soul and spirit?...". Once when I was watching Bishop TD Jakes and "The Potter's Touch", he reviewed an excerpt from the book of Hebrews in the Christian Bible which indicates these 2 things are not the same. It says:

> *Hebrews 4:12, "For the word of God is quick, and powerful, and sharper than any two-edged sword, piercing even to the dividing asunder of soul and spirit, and of the joints and marrow, and is a discerner of the thoughts and intents of the heart."*

So intrigued by this question I posed to myself and the lesson from Bishop Jakes, I set out on a quest to find the answer to the question, "what is the difference between my soul and my spirit?", I came upon a podcast at holdingtotruth.com by Tom Smith. It showed the body, spirit and soul as a

3 tiered circle with the body as the outermost layer of ourselves, the soul (which = mind and heart) as the inner tier, and the spirit (which is immortal and closest to God) as the inner-most tier.[10] Of course it's difficult to know for sure if this is true, but somehow this was an image that I could relate to...it made sense to me. I started to spend every moment I possibly could, trying to get closer to the inner-most space within me... the sacred spots. It felt warm there. I liked it. In fact, I *loved* it!

The daily practice of remembering to love myself, is reinforced as I read the Bible, as well as other documents of spiritual wisdom that I have adopted. This is a deliberate act that I now consider an absolute, non-negotiable necessity for me to stay emotionally healthy. It's not automatic. It involves a conscious working of the mind to turn yourself inside yourself. If I could spend every waking minute in this space, I would...but I'm not that good at it. Yet, I still try. The more you do it, the better you get. The ritual of daily spiritual reading and centering of self is essential for me to remain familiar with the real me, inside of me, and the purpose of that real me. Deepak Chopra refers to this person as the "authentic self " in his book, *Spiritual Solutions.*[11] This practice of "authentic self-love", if you will, has altered my life in a way that is so abundantly meaningful, I have no words to describe it. I feel like up to this point, I spent my life wandering in darkness, and now, only now, am I coming into the light and beauty of this existence.

Chapter Fourteen:

God Blesses the Mess—a Lesson in the True Meaning of Faith and Forgiveness

O ne of my good friends always says, "The bigger the mess, the bigger the bless." For a while, I kept thinking, "what good will come of all this?" How will I be blessed? What more lessons am I to learn? Well, the biggest lesson was the real meaning of faith…blind faith. People throw the word "faith" around all the time, but having faith is an extremely complicated endeavor, especially for highly intellectual people. It had to come to me over several phases. First, I listened to the book, *The Secret*[12], by Rhonda Byrne and equated its message to faith. But I found myself just imagining living in bliss with my husband again, was somewhat fairytale or what my priest calls "magical" thinking.

Don't get me wrong, I don't disregard the power of positive thinking. However, there were times when my mind was so inundated with negativity at one point, that I needed something tangible to tip my internal thought scale over to the positive side. Unfortunately, dealing with my husband head on gave me no encouragement. Every time I called him by phone, I expected him to be different, but he was still the same. He would only question me on the progress of the divorce proceedings. Each time I hung up the phone, I would be devastated, thinking it didn't work again, so I had to change my thinking. Then I started sending him quotes and reading materials about "fixing your marriage," from Mort Fertel @ marriagemax.com I guess I did it wrong, because this only irritated him. He had a different agenda, and did not want to try anything at all. So I decided that I was again, spending far too much time on trying to get him to change *his* mind, and decided to stay focused on changing *my* mind. So I would pray.

Dear God, this is a mess. I know that you wouldn't take me through this unless there's some big lesson to learn or something I must do. So please, reveal it to me…what do you want me to learn?

I asked this question for three months solid before I started to figure out the answer. Sometimes I would hear soft voices when I prayed and wondered if it was the voice of God, an angel, or if I'd really just gone completely nuts! I wondered if some messages were the slithering tongue of that which is evil in this world, so I prayed for the wisdom to be able to delineate the messages, and what I was to do with them. I went back to Rick Johnson's description of men's tendency to compartmentalize everything. That they are not mentally wired to connect complicated unrelated concepts. So I stopped expecting my husband to relate to what happened to us the way I understood it. After all, I didn't want to make him dizzy with my female reasoning. Second, Johnson also shares a quote in his book that says a happy wife loves her husband a little and understands him a lot. So I started to try to look at the world from my husband's perspective. This all happened around the same time that Pastor Joel Osteen, who I watch some Sundays before going to my own church, gave a sermon about understanding another's pain or action by listening to their story or trying to walk in their shoes. Same message of empathy, stated in a slightly different way. These little pearls of wisdom connected together gave me an insight you cannot imagine.

So I decided to try to empathize with my husband. I got inside his frame of mind and looked at the world from his perspective. It wasn't long, before I was able to become my husband, who really thinks his life is more peaceful not being married. He's also in the midst of a dynamic and booming career, which is so important to him. In Steve Harvey's book, *Act Like a Lady Think Like a Man*[13], he describes early on about men's need to be successful in career. Career is important for women as well; for us, if it doesn't work out, we just regroup and make another plan. Men take this career thing to another level. One that, being a woman, I can't really relate to. It's like indoctrinated in their soul that they should be winners in the workplace. My husband is quite successful in his career. I know he's worked very hard to achieve what he has, and I was always proud of him for his focus and determination. The success feels good to him, as it should. It feeds his image, self-worth, and self-esteem. What I've now learned is how extremely vital a good career and success are for a man. Here in lies the lesson of many great "aha's during this journey." I was no longer thinking of myself and what I wanted; I was thinking of him and what he wanted. Only then, at that moment, I realized what I just realized: It took a while, but eventually my heart began to soften, and compassion took root. I'm sure that my husband wants, what everyone does; success, peace, and happiness. He went after it, the only way he could figure out it would work at the time. He couldn't find a way, in his heart, to include me in this endeavor, in the midst of my own hectic and stressful career move. Things I said to him, hurt him in a way that he could not see a bigger picture with us as a harmonious pair. He could not see our circumstance as transient. He could not define the type of sticktoitiveness needed to endure the weight of that stressful time between us. He instead, chose to let go and travel a road without me. I realized that to really love someone, you'd want them to have what they feel they need to be happy. So, I let my husband go, not immediately, but in small stages. I had to let go of my friendship with him, my dreams of a future with him, all of what his presence represented to me in my life. I had to let go of the promise…of him. I don't know why I thought he was a promise anyway, no one promised me that anything, including him, would last forever. And I let him go because I love him and because, for whatever reason, he wanted to go. And since he seemed so very lost, I prayed for him to find his way. I realized that, at his particular crossroad of his life, he was no longer of a mind-set that he wanted to give what it took to be married with children. I know it sucks, and it may be unfair, but this is where he was. I didn't want to try to make him be someone he didn't currently have it in him to be. I just decided to accept who he was, the stage of life he was in, and to be happy that we had a memory…and let everything else go. I somehow knew, that if I wanted to give him the ultimate act of love, the act I needed to perform had to be an absolute, complete release, with well wishes and no ill intent. If I can paraphrase an interview I heard with the inspirational songstress, Plumb, who described this epiphany after dealing with her own marital issues, *"my husband is just a human after all"*. She told of how, during her marital strife, she turned things around by learning to love Jesus instead. I was moved by her testimony. I gave up my relationship with my husband, in exchange for developing a better relationship with Jesus—a most formidable companion …for the most opulent of relationships. If you think Jesus can't keep you warm at night…think again. Give Him a try. I feel like a kid walking around with the comfort of an always accepting imaginary friend, with the exception that He is Divine--not imaginary. This shift in my practice of daily living really changed so many things for me. I changed my focus of dependence from my husband to God. I then re-examined what I thought I wanted. Did having the title of "married woman" really mean that much to me, afterall? Certainly, you shouldn't want to be married to someone who doesn't want to be married to you….just to be able to *say* you're married. Sounds like more emptiness than happiness. Why should I settle for that?.

I started thinking about what unconditional love really means… For years my favorite song has been Billy Joel's, *I love you just the way you are*. That's it. The novel epiphany was that I found out that I can still love my husband for the way he is, underneath all the extras that I don't understand—the places where I know he has pain. I love the raw, untainted him that's beneath the mask and layers. In the same token, I love myself in that same way. Until I made these connections, I had no idea I had this much capacity for acceptance. When I completely engulfed the depth and complexity of this degree of acceptance, I was able to let go of what was or what didn't happen the way I'd previously thought it was supposed to. For all I know, maybe this is exactly what was supposed to happen. I found out so much about myself that I never would have known had this not occurred. And I stopped feeling like I was alone. I actually began to feel like I escaped from self-judgement, ridicule, and an imprisonment of my own soul. I was previously trapped in a phony existence completely dependent on external factors for joy and happiness. I was living in the midst of a lie, a lie about how I really felt about myself. I didn't know it but prior to this I was metaphorically enslaved.

Enslaved: I lived a life hungry for approval and validation from others. God had to break me completely open to expose my flaws, so that I could see my own internal beauty. I had to learn to accept my own uniqueness, not allowing that to be defined or tethered to any one thing or person, just the raw essence of me alone. Only then was I able to break free from that life of entrapment. Only then, did the opinions of others no longer matter. I decided to be guided solely by God's purpose for my individual life, and nothing else. Then I became free. Suddenly the world conformed to me, rather than it being the other way around.

This experience taught me to abandon that way of unfulfilling life and rely on the ever-present well of love and happiness that I carry around within. Before I felt like I was rotting from the inside out, now I am *living* from the inside out. In order to make the change, I had to go into my core, and clear out the toxic waste dump it had become. Now what springs forth is a crystal clear, self-accepted truth about myself, embracing my strengths as well as my weaknesses. I learned to live with a thankful heart for all my joys along with my pains. Not only did I forgive my husband for hurting me, but I forgave myself for hurting him and not knowing how to stop. I vowed to never hurt him ever again. I also forgave all the places in my past where evil crossed my own path and tainted my own perceptions about relationships.

I once heard on Oprah that the true way to forgive a wrongdoing and free oneself, is by letting go of what you thought should have happened. How profoundly freeing. My five-year-old once told me that to say, "I forgive you," means it never happened. Again, how profoundly freeing. So I let myself and my husband off the hook and worked very hard on removing the extraneous connotations I'd attached to our breakup. I reflected on why I was really afraid to let go. I thought things like, *What would people say? What would they think of me if they knew my husband walked out on me? Will I look undesirable or unwanted? What do my children really think? What type of marriages will they have? Will I look like a failure or loser to them or to others?* All those questions, for one, had too many *I's* and too many worries about what everybody else would think. I now recognize that these were evil-spirited seeds, planted to make me doubt myself and feel bad about myself. Even though I was becoming actively enlightened, the evil whispers of self-doubt would keep trying to seep in. I spent far too much time focusing on myself and how I'd look to other people.

It's common to run into people who will have criticisms about the way you conduct your life, but in reality, they should really stick to conducting their own lives. These commentators are also imperfect people who most assuredly will or have their own life struggle to tend to. We all must go through these rites of passage. It's part of our human existence. If you think you know someone with a perfect life, please know that you don't know their entire story. Their struggle is there, it's just not always made public. Aside from my concerns about the children, what else really mattered in the grand scheme of life? In other words, *Who cares? Who's perfect, exactly?* Let he who has no sin cast the first stone…. After all, what was going to happen to me if I got divorced? Was I going to blow up? No. Remember, that doesn't happen. When I finally learned to love the little girl inside, who grew up to be me, these questions and their answers became more and more trivial.

At some point I decided that the only thing that really mattered was having the type of human experience God intended for me to have. I wanted to live a life, out in the open, no hiding, only truth. I wanted to live a life aligned with spiritual law and use the intrinsic gifts bestowed upon me in a meaningful way. It took me close to a year of asking myself over and over, "what are my natural gifts?", "what am I good at?", "what am I here for?", "what is my purpose?". After paying really close attention, to my daily life, and contact with others, I came up with an answer. I think that my gift is the gift of *compassionate insight*. I've not previously tapped into it as much as I can now. I believe that I am to use this gift of *compassionate insight* to be a great educator and help others see what they are unable to see. With this gift I will bring comfort. This, I believe is my purpose. Whether it be, helping a patient understand their illness and how we can use modern medicine to try to fix it, helping my children navigate through the ups and downs of their young lives, or writing this book to help you, my role is to comfort. My role is to shed light on a topic in such a way that the darkness no longer appears dark. After I recognized this talent/gift, so much about my life has changed and feels more natural to me. What I am here for seems clear to me now. How I'm best suited to interact with the outside world is no longer fuzzy. It now makes sense. I now make sense. The way I approach my children, family, friends, my job, and even the person who hurt me the most, have all changed for the better. Sometimes I don't get it right off the bat, but I listen very closely, and if God reveals a way for me to help, I go that route. If there is a way, I trust that God will reveal it to me, so that I can put into use, the gifts He gave me. That level of trust, the sense of knowing that the answer will come if I pay attention, is what *faith* is all about. I keep Jesus as a close and constant companion, and use the examples He set when He walked the earth as a human being. I picture Him walking with me throughout my day. He never tires of me, judges me, criticizes me. He'll never leave me. He would never break my heart. He is the one I should have given my heart to all along—not man. Thank you Plumb for hipping me to this fact of human limitations.

Chapter Fifteen:
Faith Is Trust

I once heard a Christian psychiatrist, Dr. Tim Jennings, author of *Could It Be This Simple*[14] speak about faith. His take on "blind faith" was quite interesting. His lecture pointed out that faith really isn't blind at all. The example he gave was that of a child who has parents she trusts. If that parent tells her there is a gift for her in the closet, she has faith that they are being truthful, as they've proven themselves to be reliable and always have come through for her. Well, our Creator does the same. God comes through for us...always. All those people in my past who said that things would work out, were right. Now I ask the question differently; how do things just "somehow" work out for the best? Why do you think that is? You might as well have faith in our heavenly Father, as He doesn't let us down and really does always somehow provide. The "somehow" is one of life's great mysteries. Believing that there is a "somehow", is the *faith* part of it after all. So as my father used to say, in his Jamaican accent, "Don't fret about it". Just let it go. Let what will be...be. *'Que, Sera, Sera'*. Finally, I decided that since I really don't like feeling bad about myself, I just wouldn't. Instead, I learned to believe in the "somehow". All I needed to do was put in the work by applying a mindset of compassionate insight (a.k.a my gift) into every task or problem, and the rest would just work itself out. I tried to live in the faith of knowing that there is an answer to every question, and I don't have to have it readily available and at my disposal; it will just come. But you can't escape the work. You have to do your part. I went on with the business of re-defining my character, and tried very hard to have a non-judgmental heart about every encounter and every decision that came across my path, even in dealing with my husband. The

King James Study Bible sums this up as the principles for governing Christian conduct: (1) Live by love; (2) Live by the Holy Spirit.

Learning to walk in this new light only happened later in my journey. The more I practice honing in on the desires of my soul...the purpose of my spirit; I become stronger and more self-assured. I now know that the longer I live, the more exciting my journey will be. I almost can't wait to see what happens next; what more I have yet to discover. Thiss journey of life never ends. I will continue to build on the lessons I've learned, and use them to face new obstacles. There will always be new choices to be made. Now that I love myself and am familiar with how to continually converse with the part of God that is within me and Jesus who walks beside me, I have FAITH that I will make better choices than I have in the past. There always, always, always is a "somehow". As Deepak Chopra teaches in, *The Seven Spiritual Laws of Success*[15], it stands to reason that good choices will lead to good outcomes, and therefore good destiny. This again goes back to the *Let's Make a Deal* curtain analogy. I am now looking forward to the future, because I've learned to make better choices.

I absolutely cannot impress upon you enough, how utterly surprised I am that I could ever say that I am looking forward to the future. This feeling did not come to me overnight. I first had to go through all the bad feeling part in order to learn how to even stand upright. Learning to change my perspective was difficult at first, like swallowing some awful tasting medicine or suffering through some toxic blend of chemotherapy with an ultimate goal of cure. What I was seeking was cure of my soul...clarity of my spirit. I no longer feel like I have to ESCAPE my life to ENJOY my life. And that revelation almost brings me to my knees. I now have tools to put into use if I get even a little unsteady along the rest of my life journey. Within me there is a great wealth of experiences as well as a Holy presence to guide every decision. Since some of us humans, like to have control, it can take some time to learn to live this way. I've abandoned the need to have control over the details of all outcomes. All I have to do every day is just use my divine gifts, follow divine order, and trust that the "somehow" is out there guiding me to a good end. If I do that, then my day is a success, and feels more like an adventure or experience, than simply just another day. It takes practice, discipline, and deep thought to live from this perspective. You don't just "get it", and then you are done. You must learn to interconnect situations and circumstances in a meaningful way. For me, it requires daily ritual, constant reinforcement, guidance from the spiritual teachers around me including the Holy Bible, my priest, religious programming, and books on spirituality from multiple authors some of whom I've referred to in this book. This is a journey toward letting go; one without shortcuts or quick fixes. This journey requires diligence, and firmness of mind. This journey will bring forth your courage. If you don't want to use the tools I did, I hope you design some tools of your own, ones that make sense to you, and can help you climb out your own personal hole and heal from whatever pain you have in your life right now. Know this--The true battle is never really about the "thing" or circumstance, it's about how you handle the "thing" or circumstance. And there is always temptation looming along the road ahead to test you, almost luring you to fall back into a hole of ugliness and unhappiness. This is why I don't let up on the reinforcement—NOT EVER! I try as best I can to operate from a peaceful realm and listen with a heart of understanding. I have seen the ball of live wire within me triggered, even in this state of enlightenment. This only tells me, I still have more to learn about remaining centered and focused in my purpose. I'm just getting started so I don't expect to be a pro, like those who have studied spirituality for a lifetime. I try to remain aware of my lively ball of wire, and am practicing how to tame it when it gets triggered, so it does not tempt me to fall prey to anger or any other undesirable reaction. I'm still on the healing portion of my journey, but I now feel that I'm on the right road to having a blessed mess......

Chapter Sixteen:
A Pleasant Surprise—
Letting Go and Getting Back

So you may be hoping that this book will have a fairy-tale ending. That my husband ultimately comes back to his family, and we live happily ever after. On the other hand, maybe you've heard this we've-split-up story as the beginning of so many divorces that you've become cynical. All fairy-tale thinking aside, I don't have an ending. I consider this my new beginning. There is a little part of me that always believed that when I could truly let go of my husband, he would come back. I really wanted to let him go, to just not love him anymore, so that I wouldn't hurt anymore. I wanted him to hurt ten times more than I was hurting. After all, I felt like he cheated me out of my future, my ever-since-childhood dream of being happily married with children. I felt like he just threw away years of hard work on a whim and humiliated me in front of everyone who knew us. Every time he spoke to the children by phone and I heard him laughing in the background, or they would tell me how much fun they had visiting him, it was like salt in my wounds. I wanted to not care about him anymore, to not be affected if he would live or die, but this was so hard to do. There were so many times I wanted to hate him in peace without constant reminders of his memory, but that didn't work either. Moreover, to "hate in peace" just doesn't go together.

The truth is, none of it went together or held together when I thought of solutions laced with hate. That's not who I am. I'm a loving person by nature. Being angry just made me feel awful inside—sick and hypocritical—like I was slowly rotting at my core and festering sores were about to pop out of my face at any minute. I realized I had two choices: I could either hold on to my pain, anger, and resentment, allowing myself to rot from the inside out; or I could let go of my pain, anger, and resentment, and allow myself to heal from the inside out. I chose to heal instead of rot, which, on the surface, seems like an obvious and logical choice, but one that can be so difficult to finally make. I figured out that the only way to be truly free of that sickness was to *really* forgive him...entirely. I needed to forgive him not only for what he'd done, but for changing his mind and deciding he wanted something different—for whatever reason he felt that he wanted or needed that "different" thing, and/or "different" life. I also had to forgive him for the way he went about it. His plan was not very graceful, and his timing was absolutely horrid. Well, who's perfect? Even though friends would tell me, "It's him, it's not you!" I didn't believe it. I didn't believe it because I'm not perfect either. But then again, who is?

When something happens that is catastrophic, I think it's human nature to go back and say, "Oh, if only I had done this, gone here, stayed home, said this, not said that...." The list goes on and on. The truth is, it wasn't one thing he said or I said...he made a choice. He made a choice that was completely opposite to the character I thought I'd known him to have. I could have been picture perfect, and he could still make that choice. An even bigger part was forgiving myself for lacking the right insight back then, and not knowing what I know now about human relationships. I guess if I already knew it, I wouldn't have needed the lesson.

Chapter Seventeen:
Enlightenment

*U*p until now, I have subtly, but not openly, shared my specialty. I practice in the field of hematology/oncology, specializing in bone marrow transplantation for high risk cancers. I arrived at this career choice after travelling a long contorted path.

After completing residency, I worked in primary care, while my husband completed his residency. At one point, I worked for a healthcare system clinic and hospital, then I did house calls for homebound and hospice patients. I was later a hospitalist, worked in indigent clinics, did a few insurance physicals, and even practiced a little island medicine when my husband was stationed on Guam. I didn't realize what I was gaining as I hopped around from job to job. At the time, I thought I was just working hard so that we could eat. Now, I can see that over the years, I've had the privilege to work with many different people from different backgrounds and all walks of life in a variety of circumstances.

All of these experiences, including this pinnacle event with my husband, have shaped me into who I am today and helped propel me toward my true destiny in life. I now work with a very special and unique patient population who often have limited chance of survival with conventional treatments. I preach to my patients the value of thinking positive, loving life, appreciating the little things and not taking anything for granted, treasuring the people around them, and living each day to the fullest. How could I tell someone that to their face, and then turn around and be ugly and hateful to my husband? I couldn't. Despite everything, I never stopped loving him. In my journey, I actually learned to love my husband in a completely different dimension and capacity than I ever knew possible. I found a tender spot of empathy for him that I didn't even know existed, our entire married life. I knew I had to let him and the thought of us as a couple, completely go, and let nature take it's divine course. I just didn't know what steps to take in order to entirely let go, and I didn't know that I didn't have to stop loving him in order to not hurt anymore.

When I finally learned the ultimate lessons in true self-love, forgiveness, and faith, I was able to secure the final foothold that thrust me out of my hole of grief. After three years of mourning, I gradually woke up. Who knows what any of this was really all about? Maybe this was a journey, specifically designed for us to go through separately. Maybe my husband is going through a journey of his own that is not meant to involve me. I may never fully understand why things so unexpectedly turned out the way they did, or why he was so unhappy that he thought that the only conceivable solution was to walk away. Maybe he doesn't even know why he made that choice. In retrospect, I can see that I put a lot of pressure on him to be my eternal source of happiness. After all, I grew up believing that is what knights in shining armor do. In real life, however, that is quite a heavy burden to place on someone and far too much to expect. I now see that the first thing I should have learned was how to make myself happy. I had to sift through a lot of debris to find my own internal beauty and reason for being.

If you're trying to find happiness in the face of another person, a bottle of liquor, comfort food, or addictive drugs, you will always miss the target and come up short. None of those external factors will ever completely fulfill the desires that you have or bring the happiness you seek. They will only lead you to spiral around in circles, chasing things that shimmer with bling, and worshipping the wrong master. The "thing" becomes a false god or idol of worship. "It" will always and eventually leave you empty. It's like the crack addict that keeps doing crack trying to escape from reality and get to a place of an ultimate high that he can never reach. In worship of the crack high, he desecrates his self and his character in the process. True happiness is attained, when you learn how to mentally hone in on that place within you that bears quiet, pure happiness. Don't look to the external world to bring happiness *in*. Change your perspective to *exuding* happiness out. When you understand the beauty within your own self, it almost exudes from your pores, automatically infecting the world around you by default. Nurture the beauty that is within you. When I tapped into my own soul...my own spirit, I allowed that space within me to grow and start taking over. I felt reborn. When you learn how to nourish your internal happiness, everything tends to go more smoothly, and the one thing that you can rely on is that you won't let your own self down because you always have your own best interest at heart. I gradually learned this concept. Another key to my enlightenment, was when I stopped holding on to the idea of what was *not* happening for me in my life and changed my perspective to focus on what *was* happening for me in my life, I learned to live with a grateful heart.

I realized that all the steps I'd been taking were leading me to this place of openness. We humans think we're so in control, but we're not. There's a divine order to things. There's a pulse to everything, a heartbeat, a rhythm. This really dawned on me one day when I started off on my morning jog. I saw about 30 birds, standing at attention but facing each other, on the lawn in front of the school behind my house. They were in a weird, catty-corner formation. It was eerie. I wanted to look closer, but was actually afraid, like if I disturbed whatever it was they were doing, they might have attacked me. I briefly tried to research whether birds sleep in a V-J formation like how they migrate, but came up with no answers. I only concluded that this was some type of instinctual ritual, and they were following natural order–as all the earth does. We have the same order governing our lives as well, we just don't know it, we resist it, and we cause or own hell.

The more stories I read on the internet about couples going through separation and divorce, the more I realized how common our tale was. Not only is this a common tale, but my response of blaming myself, feeling "not good enough," ashamed, embarrassed, failure, and having many erratic outbursts is actually a common response to the grief provoked by this type of loss. Stories of others actually helped validate my feelings, made me realize that I wasn't crazy. Their stories helped me to stop blaming myself. As a result, I regained courage and reclaimed power. I was able to look at myself freely, and without judgment, I could say, "Okay, so this thing happened, now what? What are you going to do with the rest of your life? I was just wasting precious time dwelling in this funk. I decided when enough was enough. I needed to appreciate what I had going for me. I still had the same talents, career, family, and friends. It's not like a hunk of my physical being was now absent, and I was now walking around with a big gaping hole in my side because I don't bear the label of being someone's wife. I certainly wasn't born someone's wife. I'm a much better me, that I was before the event. I no longer need to hide behind a crutch to be "ok". I'm *already* OK! I made an active choice to really enjoy this one-time gift of a life and make it really count. Aside from taking care of my current batch of children, everything I'm doing in life that I find really worthwhile have nothing to do with my husband at all. I'd be doing the same things even if he never existed, because what I do now was always in my heart to do. I realized that when I labeled myself as "not good enough", I was insulting myself and God for that matter. Not good enough for what exactly? How can I ever say that who God made me to be is not good enough? It sounds ridiculous when put this way, but we do this every day. It's silly but when I was no longer the object of my husband's affection, I started thinking that I was of no importance and didn't matter. Society's subliminal messages about single women helped me form this perception. Among my co-workers, for example, if you're single, you're the topic of gossip and whispers that you have "no life", which I find quite insulting to anyone's life. How can you look at a person and declare they have a "non-life". That's just rude and disrespectful.

Believe it or not, our new cat also helped me to understand why every being "matters". We adopted an adult, orange and white-haired domestic cat named John Henry (yes, just like the steel driving man, who died with a hammer in his hand). John Henry is the sweetest, most tender, and loving creature I've ever had the pleasure to know—except for maybe when he's hungry. When he comes near you, his tenderness is contagious. It warms your heart. The world outside our home knows not of who he is, nor have any opinion about who he should be. Does that detract from his gentle demeanor? No. Does it take away the affect he has on us when he's near? No. No matter what is going on in the world, John Henry is always the same. He is like a decorative piece to the planet; with life, warmth, and an affectionate disposition. He will not be here forever, but while he is, he remains a beauty to behold and an awe-inspiring wonder; just like every one of us. I'm not talking about physical beauty. It's not the color of John Henry's coat, or the texture of his fur, it's the gentleness that exudes from his inner being that brings forth his warmth.

John Henry's left ear was snipped by the humane society. Initially I thought it was a defect. Even if it was, would it matter? Don't we all have what we think is a "defect" of some kind, whether internal, external, or both? We go through great lengths to hide, deny, or cover these up. But what if God is the only one who can seal your "defect"? What if all you have to do is open your eyes to see that God is the intricate link between what you perceive as a "defect"—and the uniqueness of your soul. Embrace your "defect(s)". You will find beauty, strength, and power paradoxically buried within them. When you overcome what you perceive "defect", you can learn to see what lies beneath the surface—what really matters and what does not matter. I think all of us living creatures here on earth are quite decorative— "defects" in tow. Collectively, we warm and flower the earth. If we could realize this, then we'd know that every life, more than matters. What if our *real* test is to realize how every life works together in divine order and that we are to discipline ourselves to follow this natural order without fail. What if, like in some of these popular dystopian novels of today, we're being challenged to understand this fundamental principle of divine order that continually alludes us because of earth's many distractions? What if our task is to fully embrace and lock into the idea of oneness, fluidity, and the natural rhythm of things. With full acceptance of our role, only then can we move into a new realm— one that moves *with* the dynamically changing world instead of against it? Then maybe we'd pass the test!

Dystopia or not, I know we all matter, and can all live better. In my journey, I'd become wiser and acquired skills that would result in a far richer future than anything in my past. No one could tell me these things until I realized it myself. And I couldn't fake it. In retrospect, it probably took a sum total of four, long years before I really believed in myself and my natural gifts. I learned how to use my deepening spirituality to navigate through everyday life and enhance the richness of every encounter. That's when things *really* started to change. I put in countless hours of mental work to find out who I really was on the inside, without the fluff. The trickiest part was that when I found who I was looking for, I was shocked to learn that I was here the whole time. I thought, *of course, now I remember. Here I am. Why couldn't I see myself?* I rejoiced when I reunited with the "me" inside of me. I looked forward to the time I spent in centering prayer, when I spent meaningful time with myself in the mindset of God and holy intention—searching deeply for my buried spirit. I can't say it enough, but this was a really big deal. When I let go of all the superficial labels, conjured expectations, and just looked at the raw, untainted inner me, I actually could see that I was good. I actually liked myself!!!! This is, by far, the greatest gift that I could ever have hoped to have in my lifetime, and it came as a complete surprise. What a revelation! I felt like I could see what moved me and why. I'm continually learning how to make choices from that space. It makes life so much less difficult living this way.

All of us have something unique about ourselves, to focus on, develop, cherish and love. We are all the flowers of the earth, remember. That thing that God put in you is *you*-nique (Ha Ha!). The circumstances that shaped you, the things that you care about, set you apart from everyone else in the world. This is the the gift *you* bring to the world. You may be a good singer, artist, or cook, a good daughter or friend. You may dance well; you may be an excellent negotiator or good listener. You may be really good with children, or have a knack for bringing people together. Maybe you're creative or crafty. You may be dependable or really good at your job, making other people happy, or you may be a thoughtful giver. You may be passionate about world hunger, religion, animal rescue shelters, or world peace. You see, you have something. All of us possess something that's unique and special about ourselves. Tap into that and use it to do something good. It's the tool God gave you when He made you for whatever purpose He intended for you. The good thing is, all of us possess the power to tap into our true calling in life, to define and mold ourselves without the requirement of anyone else's input. It doesn't matter where you are, just tap into your own natural and divine inner beauty, define your own passion, and pursue the passion you define. If you're destined to do this alongside a companion, then so be it. If not, then so be that too. With this power, you will hold the key to your own destiny, no one else.

Have you had a pinnacle event in life? Maybe you haven't experience it yet, maybe you have. Recognize it and use it. It happened for a reason. Everything does, remember. How many times have we all heard messages from very successful and influential people about the power of positive thinking, giving, and being thankful in their lives. If so many of them say it, there must be some truth to it. When I learned to flood my thoughts with positive images, positive memories, and fantasy of bliss in my future, I was finally able to "let go and let God" teach the lessons He intended for my husband to my husband, and I would concentrate on learning the lessons that God intended for me. Really, letting go completely was and continues to be by far the hardest step. People throw the term "just let it go" around all the time, but it's not so easy, because people can be really irritating, with our little struggling selves. But you have to train yourself to rise above all petty things that don't matter in the grand scheme of creation. It takes a while to figure out how to even take the first step. Without knowing what was happening to me as I acquired all the tools I used for coping, I was actually getting myself geared up to take my first step away from sadness and into long-term happiness. It amazes me that a shift in perspective from outward focus to inward focus, could transform every single aspect of my life. Every day I seem to get better at shifting back and forth to allow my inner power to project into my outer world. It still requires practice and commitment. The way I see it, my life really depends on me doing this. Sometimes, that's what it takes for a person to really change—for you to feel like your life depends on it. I still go through ups and downs, but much less often. I think to have that happen at some degree, is understandable. I just remind myself that this event in my life was not a mistake. It was an event that was specifically designed for a bigger purpose. I take each day, one at a time, which is really all anyone can do in the physical world anyway I practice living with a thankful heart for all my experiences as they've made me an insightful and thoughtful human being.

I recall an experience I had while running. I have a regular path that ends in a long steady hill leading up to my house. For about a year, I tried to tackle this hill at the end of my run. I would psyche myself up, play angry rap songs, and really try to charge this hill, but was never successful. I would always get tuckered out and only get halfway up. One day, as I approached the base of my nemesis hill, I thought, *Why do I try to charge this hill? It never works. You know, I've been tackling this hill like the hare in "The Tortoise and the Hare." I think, this time, I'll be the tortoise. After all, slow and steady won him the race, I'm sure it could work for me. There's definitely more symbolism in this story, than I ever gave any credit.* In the next breaths, I asked myself, *who am I racing against anyway? There's no one out here besides me.* As I spoke these words to myself, the incline began. I just kept thinking, *One step at a time. I can always just take one more step. One step is so easy. I can go as slow as I want to. My feet work perfectly fine. One more step is no big deal.* It went on and on, until to my surprise, I'd reach the top of the hill. I was hardly out of breath. I had *never* done that before. I felt pretty darn good. As I cooled down after that run I thought, *Running really is a metaphor for life. Wow and yay! Look at what I can do!* It seems crazy to me now, but when things started going wrong with my husband, my self-esteem crumbled down to about zero (maybe even sub-zero). I don't even know how anyone could get this low. I thought everything was my fault, and I was doing everything wrong. I felt incompetent at life in general. Nothing was right and everything was wrong. I was fairly hard on myself, scatter-brained, and irrational. I have no idea how this drastic change in my thinking occurred. Maybe I really didn't believe in myself to begin with, which is why I was hiding behind labels. That's why it was so easy to fall into thinking that I was the failure—that I'd done everything wrong because I just wasn't "good enough". I can only thank God for somehow helping me realize that I was the only person on earth who had the power to reverse that poisonous and self-defeated thinking pattern. I was the only person who could rebuild my own self, one small brick at a time, one step at a time. The ball was in my court. I had to make the choice to learn to build myself up, and stop tearing myself down. I couldn't rely on anyone else to do it, except myself. I wouldn't have believed anyone else anyway. I had to believe in myself. Starting point: subzero.

A seasoned runner once told me that practically, anyone with two working lower extremities can put one foot in front of the other, but your mental attitude about it can make you or break you. After conquering my nemesis hill, his message came to me full circle. Just as I'd previously worn my own self out trying to tackle that hill, I realized that I'd spent many years trying to "tackle" life in big chunks and great forward leaps, and somehow missed all the rich details why I did any of the things I did. Maybe I should have slowed down and tried to understand myself better, and learn how to embrace my close contacts, my surroundings, my lessons. If I wasn't always looking over my shoulder to see who was "not" trying to catch me, I might have even enjoyed the run along the way. I even tackled my grief this way. I wanted to snap my fingers and *presto!*…have it instantaneously disappear. But life doesn't work that way, does it? This mind-set was keeping me in a frustrated state of superficial thinking, making it nearly impossible for me get under the surface of things and completely heal. There are just some things you have to go through and grow through one step at a time. Taking a journey deep into the confines of your soul /spirit doesn't happen at the snap of anyone's fingers.

I think many of us have an idea that if we work faster and harder, we can get our reward quicker. We always want our results, and we want them yesterday. But we need to ask ourselves, *Does hurried mass production lead to a quality product that will be long-lasting?* Isn't it often better to take time and pride in your work? Doesn't that usually lead to a sweeter harvest? Have you ever noticed how some older people seem to do things so slowly, but somehow get so many things done (well and effortlessly no less)? I think time and wisdom taught them this lesson. Maybe more of us should pause and ask ourselves what we're really trying to win. Who are we racing? Could it be that at most times, the rat race we're running is only in our minds? Do we psyche ourselves into frenzy in a race with no other contestants? What drives us? Is it something we fear, laced in insecurity. Is that fear real or is it conceived? At times the mind can be the devil's playground. You have to train yourself to separate what is true from untrue, constant from that which is ever changing. Eckhart Tolle, author of *A New Earth,*[16] described this internal separation of thought and self in a recent interview with Oprah Winfrey on the program, *Super Soul Sunday* on her OWN network. At first it was difficult for me to conceptualize, as we are not brought up trained to think this way. It may take a moment to grasp, and requires even more abstract thought and severance of what seems inseparable, but the time spent figuring it out is well worth it. This interview put his books on the top of my "to read" list as I was intrigued by the conversation. To summarize, he talked about how your inner being is not made up of your thoughts. Thoughts can be managed as they are, more or less, just pickled by your circumstances and life exposures. Your inner being is a separate entity. It is stronger but can get drowned by the noise of thoughts when the mind is untrained to make a distinction between the two. It was after I listened to this program that I was able to start the search for my inner core being, and I found the little girl that lie dormant in the confines of my past. I don't think I would have otherwise known how to seek the truth within myself, had I not heard Mr Tolle's description of how to turn self perception around and upon itself, in this way.

Another example may be to look at the common catch phrase, "Mind over matter". Take care to know what it is your mind is showing you, because you cannot trust everything you see in your mind's eye. It can be jaded by false beliefs and circumstantial information. As you clear up your thinking, you can decide whether your thoughts are true or a distorted perception of truth. Have you ever stopped to think that life really is only as hard as we tell ourselves it is? What if everything you come across is manageable depending on how you look at it? I put this theory to the test. I decided to label every task as "easy" and "manageable." No matter how complex, I started breaking everything down into teeny-weeny tangible portions. If you think about it, everything can be broken down into smaller portions. Within time, once I found that out, I had a handle on more things in my life simultaneously and with less effort than I'd ever experienced. I found that this was the perfect way to chip away at monumental-appearing tasks that once overwhelmed and paralyzed me. When faced with a new task, my reflex reaction is to feel overwhelmed, then I remind myself to slow down, and start breaking it down. I can still hear traces of the internal lies of inadequacy that will attempt to drag me back into realm of defeat before I even get started so on a regular basis I have to keep centered to manage my emotions and stay on top of my life's tasks. When I incorporate expression of my God-given purpose into any task, it becomes worthwhile. So I try to do that with just about everything. It's always, just about how you look at it. Always.

Chapter Eighteen:
Falling Into Order

*I*t is so difficult to heal from emotional pain if you feel like your world is crumbling around you at your feet. I decided to work on myself from every angle, to set myself up for success. I always said that if I figured out the key to avoid procrastination, I'd write a book about it. Well, here it is. Taking on tasks— even my own healing—bit by bit, put my life in order. It made me feel so good and back in control. I applied this new approach to everything from preparing complicated presentations to folding laundry. I used it to muddle through the new awkwardness I had in dealing with my husband's changed personality, knowing that in time, this approach would illicit responses from him worthy of the respect that I deserved. I learned to suppress my natural instinct to react reflexively and steadied my responses to all stressors. I started to feel like the character of Neo when he finally learned the secret of the *Matrix*. In the last film of the trilogy, although he was physically blinded, he acquired the ability to see with a higher form of vision. The world became clear, and he could no longer be defeated. I felt as though I'd stepped into another physical dimension, rose above my circumstance, and started being able to see things for what they really were. Now, I use this lesson almost like a mantra. Whenever something seems "too hard" or "too difficult," or I just don't feel like doing a task, I remember that, "slow and steady wins the race", and remind myself that I have a God-given internal beauty, a meaning and a purpose here on this earth. This is what reminds me that all things are relative, including time. It reminds me to slow down, not panic, and take life one step at a time to achieve a goal. Especially when I feel afraid, I then tighten my clasp on Jesus, and we just go for it. Even when faced with the most complex tasks, I suppress my natural instinct to become overwhelmed and stressed, take a deep breath, slow myself down, focus, and just start plugging away, little bit by little bit; putting my own unique twist or touch of creativity into it. I re-member the image of myself at the top of that hill leading to my house on the day of my successful run, and I immediately gain the courage to take the first step. No matter how large or small the task, I started telling myself, *Hey...I CAN do this! There's nothing wrong with me. I am physically capable of doing this thing! If I don't know it, I can learn it!*

James Clear, one of the authors of *The Habits of Successful People[17]*, has a blog that I find quite helpful when I need more get up and go to organize my day, organize my life, organize my goals. He has an article about procrastina-tion that reminds us of Newton's law of motion—you remember—things in motion stay in motion and things at rest stay at rest. In this particular article, Clear coins the 2 minute rule in which paraphrased goes essentially like this: "If you can do something in 2 minutes, just do it and be done with it. Things that are hard to do, only take 2 minutes to get started. Once you start things, momentum will do the rest....because things in motion stay in motion...." This small morsel of information is worth it's weight in gold. It can help you overcome so many things that hold you back from getting things accom-plished. Even if it's just getting out of bed! I thank God for the very many life-coaches we have access to, who have figured out the way to do things, and are willing to help us all. Really if you think about it, there are really no *new* human problems, we just for some reason need things told to us in *new* ways. I thank God for stirring up my life in a way that forced me to release the person I had trapped inside of me. What remarkable gifts to stumble upon.

After a while, the bad days became seldom. Gradually, and I mean like snail pace gradually, the I-miss-him feeling came less frequently, and the trust in the "somehow" replaced the longing feeling in my heart. Now, my thoughts of him are followed by a quiet, gentle, and knowing smile. I have love for him, what we were as a couple, and what we are now as we grow as individuals. I think there are benefits to marriage when done right. We just didn't do it right. But I forgive us both, for not knowing any better. Now that I can see that my husband is not here, I just look over to my left, my right, over my shoulder, and inside of myself, and I see God who is within me and alongside me in every direction that I turn. Slowly and steadily, He guides my next step. Like the little girl learning to walk through the pages of my memories, I now hold my heavenly Father's hand to know the safest path to follow from this point forth, and know that the "somehow" is real and always there. As long as I always look to God and all my Godly guides, before making a decision, I am less likely to make the wrong moves and say the wrong things. I can more easily discredit negative thoughts that tend to leak out from that internal ball of loose wire

Living in an inward state of God's energy has brought me tremendous emotional strength and stability. Every morning, at the first gain of con-sciousness, I go into the quiet space that is my inner self, and recall my thoughts of the day before and thank God for what lies ahead— which all feels good now, because my perspective has changed to one of wonderment instead of grief. I celebrate for that which I am thankful, and dissect that which brought on feelings of fear or insecurity. Then I give a deep and heartfelt thanks for having arrived at this place where I can be so open and honest with myself. I'm the best friend I've ever had! No one in this world understands me better than I do. What I've come to find is that most situations that bring on fear or insecurity arise from feelings that originated from an unhealthy experience, a faulty source, or really a bunch of hogwash. I can usually then talk myself right out of it, and pray for the wisdom to conquer and master that emotion when it arises the next time. It's usually the same theme, cloaked in a different context. My adult Sunday school class read the book *Temptation*[18] by Diogenes Allen. The very first chapter talks about how to start spiritual growth. One of the things he reminds us of is the promise that **"all who seek...will find."** I had no idea the great complexity in this phrase as the depth of the seeking correlates with the depth of the answer. I find that so reassuring, full of promise, and empowering.

Initially, self-reflection may be painful itself, as we've all done things we regret and would like to bury away forever, but dare to look at those things head on. You don't have to tell anyone. Then forgive yourself for any choices you made that were unfavorable, and always try to do better the next time. Dig into what influenced your decision-making. Were you hurt? Were you looking for love? Did you have a fear of not belonging or being rejected? It's okay. I've been there too. We all have. What I found out is that I do belong, as do you. You must accept this as well as yourself, for simply being. Ask yourself who put you here the way that you are? If you connect to who made you and why, you can love the being that is you.

When we are children, we are happy just being. We find pleasure in doing whatever it is that we are doing, at any given time that we are doing it...just because. Somewhere as we grow up, we decide that just being is no longer good enough. We think that something else is supposed to happen. What that is exactly, I don't know? Maybe none of us know. That's why I think we can't find it. We're looking for whatever the "something" is in the wrong place, and need to go back to our basic essence. Many of us bring about our own unhappiness by feeding on conditioned notions about what we are lacking, and that we need "more". We need to stand out, be noticed, or be "somebody". Newsflash! You already are somebody. There's nobody like you. Check the fingerprints. You are unique. You don't have to try so hard. Tap into your talents, and you're set. Don't fear that just being you won't make you happy. On the contrary, trying to be who you *think* you want to be instead of who you are, will most assuredly make you *unhappy*. Being you, and appreciating the you who you are, will bring you the deepest happiness of all.

We've acquired a bad habit of comparing ourselves to societal standards, and then deciding that we do not measure up. But what is "society"? Is this entity we call "society" tangible? Does "society" measure up to "it's" own standards? So why does "it", whatever "it" is, get to make any rules about our internal feelings about ourselves. Should "it" be so intimate with you that you spend your lifetime looking for a contrived happiness made up by this thing called "society". This search for societal defined happiness is a futile hunt. If you can learn the beauty of self-appreciation, then you can return to loving the being that you are, just because. I am convinced that this is the best way to live life, with self-acceptance. This way you don't spend time trying to be someone else, or striving for some impossible make believe standard. Just concentrate on your own God given gifts. Everyone has them, but you must look for them to notice them, and help them to be visible in your physical world. You have to nourish them and bring them forth in order for them to blossom. And blossom, they will. I truly believe this is the way God intended for us to live. He created us to enjoy the earth, partake of its fruit, and rule over its creatures. The human existence was initially meant to be a happy one. It has always been our sin that causes us to deviate from the happy path. There will always be distractions that can cause us to detour and lead us away from happiness, but there is no way we should remain in a suffering state, just because of a little detour or two. Everyone falls off the track a few times. Pray to find your way back on. There's no need to wander around in the wilderness. We all possess the tools to work through any deviation, and get back to God's grace. Pull all those tools together from the minute you open your eyes until you lay your head down to rest. I find that just a little exercise every day and a good night's sleep keeps me even-tempered and better able to troubleshoot when things don't work out just right. It takes some work to consciously keep all the pieces of yourself in a positive vibe. Make it a point to keep your mind, your body, and your spirit healthy. I try to nourish each part of me every day all day. I don't skip days or cut corners because the risk of relapse is real, and I will not allow myself to fall back into that hole of grief again. As far as I'm concerned, that's now over and done with. It can and will be over for you, too. Keep on thinking healthy thoughts. At first, it will be hard, but if you keep plugging away at it, it will get easier. You will find that if you just work little bit by little bit to put your life back in order, it will be...in order.

To say I learned to "accept" my situation really doesn't do justice to what really happened to me. To me, to just "accept" almost sounds like a passive defeat. No one word can ever describe the tremendous, life-altering lessons I learned from this plight. Now, at age forty, I feel like a completely different person from the one I'd previously been my entire life up until this event. It is as though I've gone through a metamorphosis—all my rough edges polished cleaned, and the secret imperfections of my inner-self, contained. As I was forced to look inside myself, I actually found purpose, beauty, truth, and strength. I found new meaning in every relationship. I found honesty. I found me. Toward the latter part of this journey, I stumbled upon a page of quotations by the American poet Ralph Waldo Emerson. Although he died in the 1800s, I find many of his words to be golden truisms that transcend time. It is interesting that he was an American Transcendentalist poet of the nineteenth century. As he puts it, "Calmness is always God-like." Before what I call "my period of enlightenment," I'd prayed with fervor and vigor through anger and with streams of tears flowing down my face. Most assuredly, divinity was surrounding me then as evidenced by the support I received from the world around me. When I got to this place of calmness, however, fears slowly dissolved and tears stopped. I knew I'd really let God into my heart and was walking with Him. I would think, *Dear Lord, I get it now. How did I not know this before?* There is an old saying "If you love something, let it go, if it comes back, it was always yours…if it doesn't, it never was." Well, I guess, somewhere in my future, I'll see if my husband was ever really mine to have or if he was just a transient part of my past, a key factor in leading to my spiritual growth. I continue to pray every day that his absence will not scar our children, and they will "somehow" get what they need to thrive during visits with him and long distance phone calls. As the old saying goes, "Nothing happens by mistake, everything happens for a reason." He may have been a means for my children to be born, and they themselves are destined for some greatness or for changing the world. I don't know. Either way it goes, I feel much better equipped to handle him, after all that I've learned. My gifts, beauty, or place in this world will not diminish. Whatever it is, God has protected me and my children every step of the way through the pain, and He will see us through every step of the way to the glory that will follow. I know that now without a doubt. That's just how it goes.

Chapter Nineteen:
Prayers with Power

*W*hen I first started writing this book, my mother had a friend call me to pray with me. She prayed in a most moving and thoughtful manner. She told me that when I pray, I should present myself to God in a certain way. Changing the way I was praying, as she told me to, gave my prayers deeper meaning. She told me to just talk to God like He's a regular person. I didn't know it at the time, but this was one of the first steps I took toward personalizing God, pulling Him out of the heavens, and into the core of my being (of course, He was never *not* with me, I just never learned to look at Him up close). She told me to just ask what I want from Him, and He would listen. I later learned to listen with an ear that was aligned with the true purpose that God had for my specific life here on earth. If it is His will, and aligned with divine purpose, then what I ask shall be done. She reminded me that He would never leave me or forsake me, and that blessings were on the way. She then asked me what I wanted from God. I was stumped. If you asked me that three years ago, I'd say without taking a breath, "I want my husband back." Now, everything is different. I'm now a woman different from the one who felt abandoned and fell into a hole of despair. Now, all I really want is the wisdom and sensitivity to know how to handle whatever comes into my path, whether it be my husband, my children, patients, or even just the everyday Joe at the corner store. I asked God to speak through my lips and touch through my hands so that those I come in contact with would be able to feel His warmth. That's what I really want my life to be about—to know exactly how to help those in need of helping. My new life plan is to consult daily with God on what I should do with each day, and how I should handle each encounter. If I don't know the right words to say, I ask that He put the right ones in my heart and on my lips. I also ask that

He speak through my mouth to my children, my patients, and anyone else whom He puts in front of me for guidance. I want those who I care for to feel that level of love through my hands as I touch their bodies, as I touch their lives. I ask to be a vessel of light, to illuminate in the minds of others the reasons behind their specific disease, and how to overcome their suffering. I offer myself as a gift to them, to help them heal and offer comfort. With all of that, how can I ever go wrong? From where I sit now, the future looks brighter every day, with more encounters to have, more people to help, and problems to help solve. It literally brings me to my knees when I think about the second chance I've been graced with, to give of myself, the gifts that God has bestowed upon me, and to live a more meaningful life true to the purpose of my very existence.

Chapter Twenty:
"What lies behind us and what lies before us
are small matter compared to what lies within us." — *Ralph Waldo Emerson*

I enjoy so many of the timeless quotes of Ralph Waldo Emerson. The message that he taught was really to learn to rise above just about any uncomfortable circumstance.

My final chapter and wish for you is that you go forth, always enjoying the adventure that life truly is, and the beauty that you bring to the world around you. This beauty can continue to grow, as long as you allow it to. Good luck to you along your journey as you learn to shed whatever your pain is or was.

Since my pain had to do with my marriage, this book may be helpful to those who are also struggling with their marriages, but may help anyone who is struggling with their selves or any kind of emotional pain. If marriage is your issue, then I would advise that you seek counsel to keep your relationship healthy before you start to struggle or even before you marry. No matter where you are or why you hurt, you can have an active relationship with God in the context of your inner-self and divine purpose. This divine relationsip will help you manage any human relationship and get past any pain. Learn when your most vulnerable times are, when you're tempted to listen to streams of tainted thoughts sullied by past memories and encounters. Like cartoons of old, which depict an angel on one shoulder and a little red devil on the other, evil hides out in the recesses of your mind, waiting for an opportunity to whisper lies of inadequacy and self-destruction into your ears. I too, tried to hide from the whispers, but the problems did not go away until I directly looked at the negativity. I did not let up on myself until I completely understood the origin of my hang-ups. Once I understood where I was coming from, I could analyze my pain, and figure out how to grow past it. This took courage. As you can probably guess, I came out on the other end, actually stronger than ever before. When you understand where your demons lie, you can figure out how to win the biggest battles that replay over and again in your mind. You must equip yourself with internal safeguards, so that you don't fall prey to endless streams of negative thought. Then you can conquer these thoughts and expose them for the lies which they really are.

So flood your mind with positive input, however it makes sense to you. Mr. Emerson also once said, "A man is what he thinks about all day long." Choose what you think about. Know what to believe and what to toss into a junk pile. Ask God for protection and which tools to activate during your weakest moments. Use what you have to use, until you become internally strong. I relied heavily on my family, friends, my wonderful, loving children, and engaged in constructive physical activity and lots of inspirational reading. What tools do you have access to? Use them all. Prepare to make them readily available for battle. If this is just too hard, ask a professional to help walk you through. Some pain can be dangerous to tackle on your own. Be selective in who you choose, and remember to do your own homework about how to heal. Little by little, your internal strength will be reinforced. I know because I have moccasins. I walked the mile. I now spend increasingly more time in deep thought and internal reflection. My inner world has become a place of calm—a safe zone of comfort for me. This is now how I pray. I try to remain in this place for the majority of my awake hours and use this energy for all human interaction. Even my early morning runs evolved into a more spiritual endeavor and over time, my angry spots melted away.

There is a religious song entitled "Who will love me for me?" by JJ Heller. She sings about different scenarios of people in despair who feel unloved and some who have done wrong. All ask God, "Who will love me for me?" Ultimately, God's answer is, and forever will be, "I will love you for you; I will give you the love that you never knew." Remember, just like my mother's friend reminded me; He will never leave you or forsake you. How can He? Well, because you are of Him and He is always within you. Take care not to waste time only seeking love outside of yourself. Remember that the primary, and by far the strongest, source of love, lies within you and can overcome the negative whispers. If you learn how to access your own personal love source, the unpredictable and erratic outward actions of others can never cause you harm. Your inner love source is where God dwells and is always and ever present—the place from which you are able to give love. It is within this place that your own inner strength lies.

The situation with my husband has by far been the biggest challenge in my life. Challenges come to all of us in many forms. Eventually, you will run into one that can only be hurdled by teaming up with the supernatural strength of your Creator. Luckily, He put a divine internal compass within each of us that we can activate to help us navigate through life's pitfalls and challenges. You only have to know that it is there, and it is yours to activate and use at will. Although you may not be able to control any storm that whirls around you, the one and only thing you can always control is yourself. There will always be obstacles to face; it's almost at par for the course in this human life of ours. What makes us great is how we handle ourselves through these mini or sometimes large battles.

One day, when I'm eighty years old, maybe I'll know why this happened to me and my husband, and I certainly will know the final outcome. What will matter as I near the end of my human life, will not be who was right or who was wrong, who said this or that, who gossiped or whispered about me, or what people think of me from a distance. The people whose opinions about me, I thought, were so important all have a journey to face of their own that may also take them to challenging places. So I pray for them to have strength for their endeavors....whenever they come to their own personal crossroad of life. None of us are above these life tasks. Experiences that stretch human range of emotion are a standard. When I am called to meet my maker, all that will matter is whether or not I chose to conduct myself through life and situations the way that God wanted me to. All of us will one day have to account for our own individual actions when we meet our own personal life challenges.

I work with a very special group of nurses, who really should bear angel wings in their own right. On their office wall is posted a message that reads as follows:

"People are often unreasonable and self-centered. Forgive them anyway.
If you are kind, people may accuse you of ulterior motives. Be kind anyway.
If you are honest, people may cheat you. Be honest anyway.
If you find happiness, people may be jealous. Be happy anyway.
The good you do today may be forgotten tomorrow. Do good anyway.
Give the world the best you have and it may never be enough.
Give your best anyway.
For you see, in the end, it's between you and God.
It was never between you and them anyway".—Mother Teresa

I leave you with this message in the final chapter of this book because, at the end of the day, all of us have to look inside of ourselves to figure out what really matters on the grandest scale of life. The completion of this book marks the completion of the most challenging part of my life-changing journey and marks my final thrust out of a pit of grief. When I began writing, I did not realize that this book would help me to take another step—in fact, the biggest step— in purging me of my pain. I no longer ruminate about negative things, as all the negativity is trapped in the confines of the preceding pages. Surprisingly, and in all honesty, as I put down this book, I now feel free to leave the past behind me. As a coffin gets lowered into the ground at a burial site, I now lay this pain of mine to rest. This situation now joins the ball of wires, but bears less sting when I see my husband's face. It helps that I've now removed much of my emotional attachment to the he and I that once was. I now see him as simply a good friend of the past and empathize with what may have weakened him. We happen to have children together, but we don't share money. He has his own destiny to fill, as do I. Whatever is to be, will be. Accepting this as fact, helps me navigate through our "new" relationship without so many extraneous emotional connotations that are not our current reality. And I remind myself constantly that he's only human.

Over the last three years, I thought that as I desperately sought ways to crawl out of that hole, I was merely trying to survive. As I neared the surface, I one day realized that, along my journey, I'd inadvertently picked up life's pearls along the way. I've learned to live differently, to think differently, and to react and interact with everything and everyone, differently. When all this began, I thought that my future would be empty and full of darkness. Whenever I tried to look ahead, all I saw was a bunch of nothingness. Now, after completing this part of my life journey, I can see how bright my future will be and am so looking forward to all the goodness that will come from my new way of living, my new faith, new insight, and new appreciation for myself. I feel like I have a new spring in my step and *glide* in my stride. Even *Madea* would look at me know and say, "Hallelujah-er!" I, myself, want to shout from a mountaintop. I wrote this book not only to help myself heal, but also as a gift to you; because I don't want anyone else to hurt. I want every one of you out there to regain control of yourselves, your emotions, and your future. Believe me, this can also happen for you. I didn't believe it either, but you, too, can be delivered from whatever personal hell you're going through. Keep moving forward even if the movement is slow. Always strive for healing, and when the time is right, it will come. Maybe you won't write a book, maybe you will. Maybe you'll do something much bigger to release your pain. Reach out to people in need, share your story, and help another. We're all connected through our experiences. Remember that everything and everyone has a unique purpose. We're all here to help each other through our human life journey. We're all here to flower the earth; to bring a little pinch of our "something special" into the recipe of life.

I tried my best to give you the most tangible examples I could think of that really describe what happened to me. At some points I found it as difficult to describe as if I were asked to draw a picture of air. I know it's there. I can feel it, but I can't touch it. It's like a feeling–bathed in an emotion–wrapped up in a heartbeat—and then there's depth. Could I be any more vague? Simply put--pain is the doorway through which you can evolve into a better quality human. If I really had to sum up the steps in my awakening I would bullet point them as follows:

Step 1: Breaking point (if you have never hit a "rock bottom" event, my story may be difficult to relate to. save it for late then)
Step 2: Hungry (starving) for help

Step 3: Willingness to change **everything** about the way I looked at **everything**

Step 4: Looked for examples of how other people heal or survive tragedy

Step 5: Figured out how I tick, what ticked me, and why.

Step 6: Separated my junky thoughts from true self—separated my spirit from my soul.

Step 7: Figured out what was important to both my soul and spirit–what moved me deeply—just me—no one else. This is what I was born for. This is what I used to approach my new world.

Step 8: Realized that I like myself, and I like, liking myself.

Step 9: Knowing that what I stood to gain by living in this new way was worth sticking around for.

I hope all of this helps. I wish you all the best.

The End...
or more appropriately; A new beginning!

References

1. Hertzler, J., *Seven stages of grief. Journey through grief.com-where pain and beauty mingle.* Retrieved December 2012 from http://www.recover-from-grief.com/7-stages-of-grief.html
2. Meyer, Stephanie. *New Moon.* New York: Little, Brown, 2006.
3. Divorce.com, *Your Divorce. Before During After.* Retrieved December 2011 from http://www.divorce.com/article/divorce-statistics
4. Bstan-'dzin-rgya-mtsho. *The Dalai Lama's Little Book of Wisdom:.* Charlottesville, VA: Hampton Roads, 2009.
5. Johnson, Rick. *Becoming Your Spouse's Better Half: Why Differences Make a Marriage Great.* Grand Rapids, MI: Revell, 2010.
6. Gray, John. *Men Are from Mars, Women Are from Venus: A Practical Guide for Improving Communication and Getting What You Want in Your Relationships.* New York, NY: HarperCollins, 1992.
7. Connor, Pat. *Whom Not to Marry: Time-tested Advice from a Higher Authority.* New York: Hyperion, 2010.
8. Eker, T. Harv. *Secrets of the Millionaire Mind: Mastering the Inner Game of Wealth.* New York: HarperCollins, 2005.
9. Dyer WW. *The power of intention: learning to co-create your world your way.* Carlsbad, Calif.: Hay House; 2004.
10. Smith, Tom. *"What Is the Difference between the Soul and the Spirit?".* Retrieved March 2015 from http://holdingtotruth.com/
11. Chopra, Deepak. *Spiritual Solutions: Answers to Life's Greatest Challenges.* New York: Harmony, 2012.
12. Byrne, Rhonda. *The Secret.* New York: Atria, 2006.
13. Harvey, Steve, and Denene Millner. *Act like a Lady, Think like a Man: What Men Really Think about Love, Relationships, Intimacy, and Commitment.* New York: Amistad, 2009.

14. Jennings, Timothy R. *Could It Be This Simple?: A Biblical Model for Healing the Mind*. Hagerstown, MD: Review & Herald Pub., 2007

15. Chopra, Deepak. *The Seven Spiritual Laws of Success: A Pocketbook Guide to Fulfilling Your Dreams*. San Rafael, CA: Amber-Allen Pub., 2007.

16. Tolle, Eckhart. *A New Earth: Awakening to Your Life's Purpose*. New York: Plume, 2006.

17. Clear, James. *How to Stop Procrastinating by Using the "2-Minute Rule"*. Retrieved March 2015 from http://jamesclear.com.

18. Allen, Diogenes, and Diogenes Allen. *Temptation*. Cambridge, MA: Cowley, 1986.